REVISED & UPDATED

COACHING YOUTH
BASKETBALL

THIRD EDITION

The Guide for Coaches, Parents and Athletes

John P. McCarthy, Jr.

FOREWORD BY SKIP PROSSER
HEAD MEN'S BASKETBALL COACH
AT WAKE FOREST UNIVERSITY

BETTERWAY BOOKS
Cincinnati, Ohio

11 10 09 08 07   6 5 4 3 2

Distributed in Canada by Fraser Direct, 100 Armstrong Avenue, Georgetown, ON, Canada L7G 5S4, Tel: (905) 877-4411. Distributed in the U.K. and Europe by David & Charles, Brunel House, Newton Abbot, Devon, TQ12 4PU, England, Tel: (+44) 1626 323200, Fax: (+44) 1626 323319, E-mail: postmaster@davidandcharles.co.uk. Distributed in Australia by Capricorn Link, P.O. Box 704, Windsor, NSW 2756 Australia, Tel: (02) 4577-3555.

Library of Congress Cataloging-in-Publication Data

McCarthy, John P., 1947-
  Coaching youth basketball : the guide for coaches and parents / John P. McCarthy, Jr. -- 3rd ed.
      p. cm.
  Includes index.
  Rev. ed. of: Youth basketball. c1996.
  ISBN-13: 978-1-55870-790-0 (pbk. : alk. paper)
  ISBN-10: 1-55870-790-5
  1. Basketball--Coaching. I. McCarthy, John P., 1947- Youth basketball. II. Title.

  GV886.25.M37 2006
  796.323207'7--dc22   2006012845

Edited by Michelle Ehrhard
Designed by Grace Ring
Illustrations by John Rizzo
Cover design by Sean Braemer and Claudean Wheeler
Cover photography by Christine Polomsky
Production coordinated by Robin Richie

ABOUT THE AUTHOR

Jack McCarthy, like many Americans, is a sports enthusiast and has played and coached numerous sports all of his life. As a parent, and now grandparent, he knows that athletic competition builds self-confidence in young people. It also prepares them to handle life's challenges and teaches them how to succeed. The Betterway Coaching Kids series was developed by Jack to help parents and coaches ensure that their child's experience in sports is a positive one.

Jack is an attorney and works for the New Jersey Courts. He lives with his wife and family, which includes three children and four grandchildren, in Hillsborough, New Jersey. His other books in the series include titles on baseball, soccer, basketball and football. He has also written *Baseball's All-Time Dream Team*.

DEDICATION

To my grandchildren, John Connor McCarthy, Shannan Adele McCarthy, Erin Kathleen Liddy, and Meghan Casey Liddy
May there always be a dream in your heart and the courage to go for it!
With love. PaPaJack

ACKNOWLEDGMENTS

Many thanks to the photo models: Megan Allen, Nicole Florentino, Joey and Jack McCarthy, Melissa Poch, Steffanie Shoop. Also to Christopher Brennan, Marshall Beveridge, Patrick Carey, Scottie Demarest, Bill Liddy, Meghan and Erin Liddy, Cole Lipman, Connor and Shannan McCarthy, Kristine McCarthy, Lynn McCarthy, Lauren Serritella, and Renee Sigler.
Well done!

TABLE OF CONTENTS

Find out why this is a great game. Begin with the basics, including the history and lingo of basketball, its rules, court dimensions, and equipment.

Understand the basketball positions: center, forwards, and guards. Learn the nature of each position, primary duties, and specific position drills. This chapter also addresses differences between boys and girls in basketball.

Learn about the top ten mechanics and dynamics of shooting, including outside, inside, and foul shots, plus shooting drills that will help players improve.

Discover the top ten keys to successful dribbling, pivoting, faking, and feinting. Use the featured dribbling drills to teach and improve these skills.

Develop and improve your players' skills with the top ten fundamentals of completing and receiving passes, and discover passing drills to use with players of all skill levels.

The offensive zones, top ten offensive concepts, multiple play patterns and drills covered in this chapter will provide a solid foundation for your team's practice and play. Pick the offense for the level of your team: beginner, intermediate, or advanced.

FOREWORD

By Skip Prosser, Head Men's Basketball Coach at Wake Forest University

Coaching is teaching. As the basketball coach at Wake Forest, I consider myself part of the faculty. While Wake Forest is one of the truly outstanding academic universities in America, I want our players to feel as though they have learned more in my "classroom" than at any other on our campus.

Coaching Youth Basketball is a book about teaching the fundamentals of the game. Our game is played by the best athletes in the world. Playing basketball is fun. But, as I tell my players, if you don't possess the proper fundamentals, you have little chance for success. An analogy would be comparing these fundamentals to tires on an automobile. You may own the most expensive automotive machine on the market, but if you have no tires, you are going nowhere. So, too, with the fundamentals of basketball. If you want to travel to the highest levels of this great game, you must possess the fundamentals. These fundamentals will take you to the top.

Coaching Youth Basketball is a must for anyone involved in instructing the basics of the game. The book takes you step by step through all of the teaching progressions that are invaluable as building blocks to improve your skill level as well as your game knowledge. All aspects are covered from a glossary of terms to diet to advice for parents. This book is a must for those who want to learn more about teaching, coaching, and playing basketball.

Today's youth have potentially more "distractions" than at any other time in our history. Many of these distractions are counter-productive to the proper mental and physical development of our children. Athletics, without question, can teach positive lessons about the rewards of hard work and selfless sacrifice for the betterment of the team. These are life lessons. To be successful eventually, both personally and professionally, you have to work at it as well as being unselfish. This book teaches us how to best instruct young people so that they can not only be successful in the game of basketball but, more importantly, be successful in the biggest game of all—the game of life!

PREFACE

"Dad, I'd really like to get a lot of playing time next year, maybe even start in some varsity games." I could see how serious my son Jack was. He had played some basketball in grammar school but had not made the freshman team in high school. As a sophomore, he was given a chance. He began to show his ability and got good "playing time" on the J.V. team. Unfortunately, halfway through the season, he slipped while rebounding and broke his wrist.

He really wanted to contribute to his team the next year, but he knew he needed to improve a lot and make up somehow for lost experience. "Okay," I said. "Let's go for it. I'll coach you this summer." I had played the game my whole life and knew I could help develop his skills. It worked out great! Jack made a major improvement, and I had the best parenting and coaching experience of my life.

It was the summer of 1984. We worked nearly every day. At first, we concentrated on dribbling and practiced a lot of jump shots. We played a lot of one-on-one to refine his offensive and defensive skills. Our family took a four-week trip across country that summer. The rest of the family would groan, as we spotted a basketball court on a prairie in South Dakota and pulled over for a quick forty-five minutes of practice. We practiced once in 110-degree Texas heat!

I would start under the basket and feed Jack rebounds for ten- to fifteen-feet jumpers until his arms nearly fell off. He would dribble with eyes closed, speed dribble thirty-yard dashes, jump rope, pass against a wall at a close distance, and shoot fouls until he was exhausted.

That year, no one could believe his improvement! He played a lot, and he started some varsity games by the end of the season. This was a boy who was cut as a freshman! What's my point? A parent can make a difference!

I also coached my younger son, Joe, in a clinic program for beginners. There, I learned a lot about what kids need to do before they can become competitive. Remember, 85 percent of kids who play in grammar school or clinics will never play for their high school team. If they learn the game, though, they will play in lots and playgrounds for their whole lives. Get players to just hang in there until they learn the basics, and they will play this wonderful game for the rest of their lives.

You don't need to be a former (or current) basketball player to be a coach or the parent of an aspiring player. Experience helps, but it's not necessary. This book will teach you all you need to know. Even if you do not want to coach formally, or if you're not athletically inclined, you can have a catch, feed rebounds, and be a companion to a child. This book will show you what to look for, as well as how to spot errors in form. Most importantly, this book will focus on concepts, so you and your young players can understand the why of things.

It's all here in this book. I have presented it in a way that a beginning coach or a parent who knows little about the game can nevertheless understand the concepts. Yet this book is not just for beginners. The seasoned youth coach will get new insights into how to improve his approach. I focus on those things that can most quickly improve a player's chances of getting some quality playing time. The book also includes a full technical review of the game, and is thus useful for coaches and players at all youth levels. Good luck with it.

To kids,
Jack McCarthy

THE GAME OF HOOPS

ENCOURAGE YOUR CHILD TO PLAY

More than for any other sport, I find myself encouraging parents to get their child involved in basketball. It just may be the best all-around game there is. Why? Well, unlike most sports, you can play hoops year-round. Outdoor courts are usually readily available, and pick-up games are easy to find, even if just a three-on-three match. During winter in northern states, school gyms or YMCAs are available. Basketball is also great for body conditioning. Best of all, you can play for your whole life. I've got four grandchildren and still enjoy the game! No other sport can boast *all* of these benefits. It's just a great game, so kids should be encouraged to play and learn basketball when they are young. The goal is not necessarily to become a star … just to get enough skill to play with confidence. They will be rewarded with a lifetime of fun, physical health, and great camaraderie.

Kids who play basketball will also gain the important life lessons of athletics. The greatest lesson is teamwork, being a team player, which is so essential in the business world today. They will learn that we all have strengths and weaknesses, how to deal with their own, and how to tolerate others'. They will learn to respect racial diversity, to understand the nature of competition, and to see how "bottom lines" relate to success. They will learn to win and lose and will win or lose enough times to know how to do both with dignity. They will appreciate the value of physical conditioning, practice, and game fundamentals. These lessons provide a youngster with rock-solid support as they go on to face the many challenges of today's world.

This book is written for coaches, parents, and players—both boys and girls—at all levels of Youth Basketball, from beginning to advanced. No matter what your players' ages, it's always smart to assume nothing and begin with the basics.

1

1-1. HOOPS: A GAME FOR ALL AGES

Whether it's little kids playing ball ...

Or big kids playing ball.

THE LINGO OF HOOPS

Teaching basic terminology is a good way to start. It helps instill confidence in young players. A grasp of the game's jargon will remove some of the fear of the unknown. The knowledge will also help players start the journey to that point where confidence replaces self-concern, where their perspective turns outward to the team and to the game instead of inward—where they are worried about themselves, how they look, or whether they are doing okay.

I coached a clinic for seven- and eight-year-olds one year and was surprised to see how little the kids knew of the lingo, the language of basketball. They knew even less about the rules. Sure, they had all heard of a slam dunk, but that was about it.

So before each practice, we sat around in a circle and went over some new words or phrases like key, foul, walk, free throw, double dribble, three seconds, jumper, and lay-up. There are dozens and dozens of words and phrases that are unique to basketball. Do about ten words at each practice. First, I'd ask them to raise their hand if they knew the word, and then I'd ask them to explain to the team what it meant to get a dialogue going. After this, we would quickly review the words from the prior practice.

It's important for players to be familiar with the basic terms. Sure, eventually they will get the lingo, but some kids get embarrassed when their ignorance is the basis for the day's lesson. You can avoid embarrassment by going over a few terms daily with your players. Be sure to read the Glossary at the end of this book; have parents read it. It covers the most important terms, giving ready definitions for each, and it will be an invaluable aid for teaching the jargon of basketball.

THE HISTORY OF HOOPS

While the language of hoops is essential to coaching and learning the game, basketball's history is fun to know. Surely, kids have been bouncing, kicking, and throwing round things for as long as there have been kids and round things. However, basketball seems to have a fairly definite point of invention.

THE INVENTOR OF BASKETBALL

In 1891, a YMCA gym teacher in Springfield, Massachusetts, Dr. James Naismith, was trying to find something more interesting for his students to do during the winter months. So he nailed two peach baskets onto a balcony, which just happened to be ten feet high, at either end of gym floor. There were eighteen players in the class, nine on a side.

Dr. Naismith typed up a list of thirteen rules. The ball, a soccer ball, could be advanced by throwing or batting it with the hands. Players could not run with the ball but had to throw it from where they caught it. No physical contact was allowed. Dribbling was not introduced until some time later, when a trapped player was allowed to throw the ball up and catch it. Floor dribbling came along even later.

THE GROWTH OF BASKETBALL

The game was an immediate success. Women started playing almost right away, in 1892, but in far fewer numbers than men. During the early years, scores were low, usually well under ten goals per game. Colleges picked it up after the turn of the century. The sport grew most rapidly in the Midwest.

STANDARD RULES

Basketball rules were standardized in the 1920s and 1930s. Free throws were no longer awarded for traveling violations, and center jumps were no longer required after each goal. The game opened up. Fast breaks and other strategies made it quicker. The first national collegiate tournament, the National Invitational Tournament (NIT) was played in 1938 (Temple 60, Colorado 36), and the NCAA tournament followed in 1939 (Oregon 46, Ohio State 33).

BASKETBALL TURNS PRO

Professional basketball started early also, in New York and New Jersey, with local teams inviting teams from other towns to play. Leagues soon followed, developing from 1906 to 1920. In 1949, the National Basketball Association developed out of inter-league competition. That year, Minneapolis, led by the great George Mikan, defeated Syracuse for the championship, six games to two. Over the years, great superstars have won the hearts of fans—Kareem Abdul-Jabbar, Wilt Chamberlain, Bob Cousy, Bill Russell, Elgin Baylor, Bob Pettit, Pete Maravich, Oscar Robertson, Rick Barry, Jerry Lucas, Magic Johnson, Michael Jordan, Larry Bird, and Shaquille O'Neal. Current all-stars such as Tim Duncan and LeBron James now vie for such basketball immortality. There are so many more of them, the all-time greats of basketball. The Women's National Basketball Association (WNBA), which started in 1997 and is backed by the NBA, is growing solidly, and the superstar list now also includes such greats as Sheryl Swoopes, Cynthia Cooper, and Lisa Leslie.

The Age of Women's Hoops

Prior to the 1970s, few schools offered girls basketball as a varsity sport. Now girls achieve near equality with boys, regarding the opportunity to play.

Why? In 1972, Title IX of the Education Amendments banned sex discrimination in schools, whether academic or athletic. Title IX says:

> "No person in the United States shall, on the basis of sex, be excluded from participation in, be denied the benefits of, or be subjected to discrimination under any educational program or activity receiving Federal financial assistance...."

As a result, colleges are required to provide women with the same opportunity, facilities, equipment, and scholarships—all the benefits given to the men's programs.

International Basketball

The International Basketball Federation (FIBA) for amateur players was formed in 1932 by eight founding nations. Basketball was first included in the Olympics in 1936, although a demonstration tournament was held in 1904. This competition has usually been dominated by the United States, whose team has won all but three titles; the first U.S. loss in a controversial final game occurred in 1972 against the Soviet Union. In 1950, the first World Championships for men were held in Argentina. Three years later, the first World Championships for women were held in Chile. Women's basketball was added to the Olympics in 1976, with teams such as Brazil and Australia rivaling the American squads.

FIBA dropped the distinction between amateur and professional players in 1989, and, in 1992, professional players played for the first time in the Olympic Games. The United States' dominance briefly resurfaced with the introduction of their Dream Team. However, with programs developing elsewhere, other national teams have now caught up with the United States. A team made up entirely of NBA players finished sixth in the 2002 World Championships. In the 2004 games, the United States suffered its first Olympic loss while using professional players, falling to Puerto Rico and eventually coming in third.

BASKETBALL'S BASIC RULES TODAY

Modern basketball is a simple game. Popular games have to be simple, since complex rules just spoil the fun of things.

A CAPSULE DESCRIPTION OF THE GAME

Two teams of five players each try to score goals by shooting a 28 1/2-inch to 30-inch round, inflated ball through one of two eighteen-inch-diameter, cylindrical hoops. These hoops are ten feet from the ground at both ends of a rectangular floor. Every game begins with a jump ball at the center of the court. With one player from each team positioned in the midcourt circle, a referee tosses the ball high into the air, and the two players attempt to tap the ball to one of their own teammates. The team that gains possession of the ball plays offense, and the opposition plays defense, protecting its own basket until it regains possession of the ball. A player can advance the ball only by passing to a teammate or by dribbling (bouncing) it continuously on the floor. Play continues, unless the ball goes out-of-bounds (the last team to touch the ball loses possession), until a goal (one, two, or three points) is scored. A goal shot is worth two points, or three points if it is shot from beyond the three-point distance (19.9 feet from the hoop for youth and college ball). Each successful foul shot scores one point. When a player from each team has a hand on the ball (called a jump ball), play is stopped. Possession in such cases is awarded alternately to each team. A possession arrow on the scorer's table indicates which team's turn it is to get the ball. The arrow changes after each jump ball. Most youth games take about sixty to ninety minutes and are divided into four quarters of six minutes each in grammar school and eight minutes each in high school, with a ten-minute half-time break. The team with the most points at the end wins.

COMMON RULES VIOLATIONS

Play also stops upon a rules violation. A common violation is walking (also called traveling)—taking more than one step without dribbling the ball. The penalty for traveling is to award possession to the opponent. Another common violation is a foul—initiating illegal physical contact with an opponent. Fouls are usually committed by a defender but may be committed by the offense, in which case they are called a charge (or player-control foul). When a foul occurs, the ball is awarded to the other team, unless the fouled player was shooting, in which case that player may shoot two free throws. When a team commits its seventh foul in a half-game, free throws are awarded to the opposing team for non-shooting fouls, and a second bonus shot is allowed if the shooter makes the first. This is known as one-and-one. When a team commits its tenth foul in a half-game, the opposing team shoots two fouls shots for that foul and for each subsequent foul. If a player accumulates five fouls in a game, he fouls out and must leave the game and cannot reenter, even if the game goes to overtime.

MORE RULES OF THE GAME

Okay, let's dig a bit deeper. Here are some more key rules which should be commonly understood. Be sure to check out the glossary for others.

1. Five players must start a game, but as few as two can finish it. The latter situation is highly unusual but could occur due to injury and/or ejection of players.
2. After a goal is scored, the ball may be in-bounded (passed into play from out-of-bounds) from any point along that end line of the court (the player inbouding the ball is free to run along hte baseline). A player has only five seconds to inbound a ball. If the ball goes out-of-bounds without a goal being scored, a player must inbound from the spot designated by the referee. Aggressive defense here can give quite a payoff because the five-second rule may pressure a player to inbound before a receiver is open.
3. A player may only dribble with one hand at a time. Kids, especially beginners, tend to bring the second hand in to help out, and that's a double-dribble violation. Once a player ceases to dribble by grasping or touching the ball with both hands, she may not dribble again.
4. A player or team has five seconds to inbound a ball and then ten more seconds to advance the ball upcourt past the division (mid-court) line. Once the ball and both of the dribbling player's feet are past that line, the backcourt (the half of the court now behind him) becomes out-of-bounds for the offense for the remainder of that possession. Teams on the defensive often employ a full-court press, meaning they attack

1-2. COMMON RULES VIOLATIONS

Inbound Pressure: Offense has five seconds to inbound the ball or lose possession, unless a time out is called.

Double-Dribble: A common mistake for closely guarded beginners is to use the free hand to help control the ball, which results in a double-dribble violation. Players should keep their free hand away from the ball.

Shooting Foul: A very common foul is for a player to strike a shooter's arm in the act of shooting.

Reaching In: Reaching in is another common foul. Stress to your players that when they go for the ball, they must not make contact with the offensive player's body.

the opponent in the backcourt area to slow them down. They are awarded the ball if ten seconds elapse before the opponent crosses the mid-court line. Most beginner leagues prohibit the press, since young dribblers have so much difficulty with it.

5. A closely guarded player can't hold or dribble the ball in place for more than five seconds, or she loses possession of the ball.

6. No part of an offensive player can remain within the offensive free-throw lane (the twelve-foot-wide rectangle directly under the basket) for more than three seconds. The tall players, such as the center, like to hang out directly under the basket, and the three-second rule prevents their hogging this valuable turf.

7. Illegal contact between opposing players is a foul. Many fouls occur when a defender tries to block a shot and hits the shooter's hand or bumps her with the body. Another common foul occurs when a defender reaches in to swat the ball and makes contact with the dribbler. (See figure 1-2.) Note that merely touching a player, "feeling" where they are, or incidental contact, is not a foul.

8. The boundary lines around the court are part of the out-of-bounds area, and if a player is in possession of the ball, neither the ball nor that player's foot may touch the line.

9. If a defensive player touches a shot ball in downward flight, goaltending will be called, and points are awarded as if the shot had been made. This rarely happens in youth ball; you will also rarely see a dunk at this level.

10. Players may not try to disconcert a free thrower. Once the free thrower has the ball, no one may enter or leave a marked lane space. Players may not enter the free-throw lane to rebound until the ball leaves the shooter's hand. The shooter may not enter the lane until the ball hits the rim or backboard.

11. According to the principle of verticalization, although a defensive player does have a right to the space directly over him and may jump straight up to block a shot without fouling, most referees will nevertheless call a foul on the defender if he makes contact with the shooter. The best advice to give your players is, when on defense under the hoop, hold their ground, raise their hands, and stay still.

12. If the shot is released before the buzzer sounds to end any period of play, the shot scores a goal even if it goes through the hoop after the buzzer sounds.

HOW TO GET MORE INFORMATION

I've presented only a thumbnail sketch of the game's main points in this chapter. This is enough to get going. There are other frequently used rules, which I'll cover later, and some minor rules, which are described in the glossary along with the jargon of the game. You can order a book outlining official basketball rules from the National Federation of State High School Associations, Box 361206, Indianapolis, Indiana 46236-5324, 1-800-776-3462, for a cost of $6.75 plus shipping. Look them up at www.nfhs.org for a lot of interesting information.

PLAYING TIME

No more than five players from each team are allowed on the floor at any one time, with youth teams usually numbering between twelve and eighteen players. This means a lot of kids either won't make the team or won't get much playing time. Fortunately, below sixth or seventh grade, and sometimes all the way up to high-school age, most towns run clinics or in-town recreation programs that provide some coaching and organized ball that allow anyone who wants to play to do so. Most of these clinics limit team size to nine or so, and often fewer players show up at each game. Such clinics usually require equal time or at least a certain minimum time for all players. Substitutions generally occur in clinic play at the end of a period, and usually a whole team is substituted for the players on the floor. At more advanced level play, substitutes enter only upon stoppage of play and must report to the scorer and referee.

I like the clinics for a number of reasons. With determination, dedication, and practice, even kids who do not get their height or coordination until much later than others can eventually compete with the more natural athletes. Very often the kids who start varsity in high school were not the best players at the grade-school level. Without the "equal opportunity" offered by public clinics, many young players would never realize their potential. Grade-school teams and many traveling programs do endeavor to get all or most kids into a game, but this varies greatly. Check to see what the policy or rules are for a program's playing time before you sign up your child. It may be in their better interest to play at a level where they will get significant playing time. It may also be that your child needs to work harder to earn that playing time. If you didn't read the preface to this book, do so now. It will tell you how to help him earn that playing time.

ON HEIGHT

The old adage is that basketball is a "big man's" game. This is an overstatement and is certainly not the case at the early youth level, where good dribblers dominate. However, there is no question that height helps a lot when defending or shooting underneath the hoop, and the highest percentage shots *are* from underneath the basket. When you get down to it, though, that's about all you need height for. Frankly, rebounding has more to do with positioning than with height. Also, at the young ages, the height differential is usually much less than it is for adults. The point I'm making is that you should not discourage a child from playing basketball if she is not tall. It's a game she can enjoy for her entire life, so urge her to learn it. The shortest player ever to play in the NBA was Muggsy Bogues, at 5' 3". Another was Spud Webb, 5', 7" tall, who had an amazing 42-inch vertical leap that gave him significantly more height when jumping.

So while height is a very important element, speed, agility, leadership, a good outside shot, good dribbling, good passing, aggressiveness, and quickness are also needed and can compensate for stature. Often, the tall youths have only their height and are otherwise less coordinated since they grew so fast. Believe me, I know. I was one of them. I must repeat, basketball is a game your children or players can enjoy their entire lives. I've played it all of my life and still do. It's a great game, good exercise, and a super way to meet people. Encourage players to hang in there and play for a few seasons. Even if a kid is not playing much, she is practicing and learning the game. This experience alone will let a child join in playground pickup games for the rest of her life.

THE COURT AND EQUIPMENT

Basketball court sizes will vary depending on the age of players and the size of available gymnasiums. Many older middle-school gyms are about half the size of the usual 50' by 84' high school courts, although newer schools now have gyms approaching or equal to high school sizes. (See figure 1-3.)

The backboard is a rectangular or semicircular, fan-shaped surface on which the basket is mounted. It is also referred to as a bangboard or bankboard because of its use for bank shots. It is also called the *glass*, if it's made out of that material. In outside lots, it's usually made of wood or metal.

The basketball itself is usually leather. The circumference must be 29.5 inches to 30 inches for boys and an inch less for girls. A basketball's weight is 20 to 22 ounces for boys, 2 ounces less for girls. The ball should be inflated to a pressure so that it will bounce to a height of 49 to 54 inches when dropped from more than 6 feet high.

BOYS AND GIRLS: A GENDER GAP?

Title IX removed the economic and other barriers to female sports. Obviously, there are still some natural differences, primarily respecting physical strength. Actually, strength

1-3. THE BASKETBALL COURT

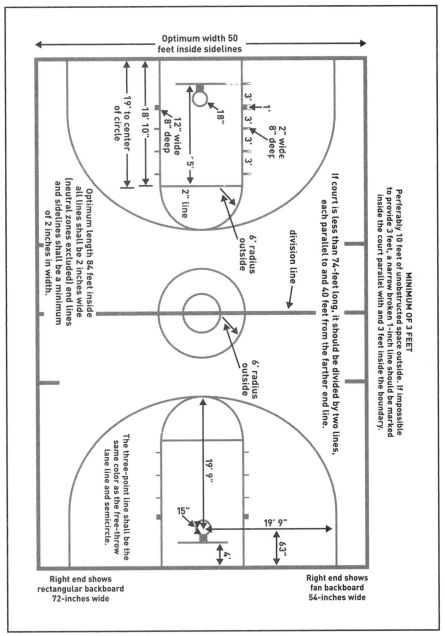

Optimum width 50 feet inside sidelines

19' to center of circle

18' 10"

12" wide 8" deep

18"

1'

3'

3'

3'

3'

2" wide 8" deep

'5'

2" line

6' radius outside

division line

Optimum length 84 feet inside all lines shall be 2 inches wide (neutral zones excluded) end lines and sidelines shall be a minimum of 2 inches in width.

6' radius outside

MINIMUM OF 3 FEET
Perferably 10 feet of unobstructed space outside. If impossible to provide 3 feet, a narrow broken 1-inch line should be marked inside the court parallel with and 3 feet inside the boundary.

If court is less than 74-feet long, it should be divided by two lines, each parallel to and 40 feet from the farther end line.

The three-point line shall be the same color as the free-throw lane line and semicircle.

19' 9"

15"

19' 9"

4'

63"

Right end shows rectangular backboard 72-inches wide

Right end shows fan backboard 54-inches wide

This diagram shows the layout of the typical 50' x 84' high-school gym.

11

is fairly close for boys and girls of equal size until they are about eight or nine years old, but after that, boys start getting much stronger. For that reason, boys and girls will likely continue to play separately, except in some exceptional circumstances. However, frankly, there are few other differences. Boys' and girls' hoops can be better characterized by the many similarities the kids exhibit regarding on-court speed, agility, aggressiveness, floor vision, and shooting. In all these skills, girls are right there with boys. Girls tend to have less experience since girls are not encouraged at very young ages to play neighborhood ball, and so they may *seem* to develop more slowly. However, take a look at college or pro hoops for women, and it is clear that all skill sets are fully developed and readily apparent. Some of the most aggressive and passionate kids I have coached have been girls.

So, from a coaching or parenting point of view, the lessons, skills, and approaches set forth in this book apply equally well to boys' or girls' teams. The game of hoops is basic and fairly straightforward, and it simply does not distinguish between the sexes.

That is not to say there aren't some differences. There are, and it is important to be aware of them.

WOMEN COACHES

A major problem is that far too few coaches today are women. Sure, it's much better than ten to twenty years ago, and more women who played youth ball are now volunteering. My daughter-in-law was a very good high-school player, and she now coaches my granddaughter. But the fact remains: We need several times more women coaches than we now have.

There is obviously no rule that female athletes must be coached by female coaches. Many men have successfully coached female teams at all levels. Why do we need women coaches? Well, some of the reasons are just obvious! We know intuitively, and research has clearly demonstrated, that the psychological make up of girls and boys is different. Their life experiences are categorically different. If we agree that effective coaching is as much about mental preparation as it is about physical preparation, then the need to understand how an athlete mentally approaches the game becomes evident. A female coach will understand the thinking and feeling processes that girls bring to the game and be able to address this difference more easily and at least make the experience a more positive one.

MOTIVATION: RELATIONSHIPS VS. STATUS

Research suggests that girls are more motivated by relationships and boys by status. Girls fear isolation from the others while boys fear looking badly, or embarrassing themselves. My own experience confirms this, and I assume it arises from the way we

1–4. **WOMEN COACHES**

Former women players are coming out in larger numbers, but still are only a small percentage of what's needed.

raise boys and girls in society. I recall coaching a girl's team once, and it seemed that, at least once a week, I'd see a player walk off or come to tears because of some thing a teammate said, particularly if a clique had formed. I wondered how I would ever get these girls working together as a team with this going on. I really agonized over this for a long time, and perhaps if I were a woman, I'd have figured it out sooner.

So, I eventually held a team meeting, and we talked about what a team was and how important teamwork was to our success. The best way to become a team would be if we all began to care more for each other, or at least try to! I said that we had a decent team, but we'd have no chance if we kept dividing ourselves up or picking on one another. If we wanted to succeed, we had to get beyond the petty stuff.

My talk seemed to fall flat at first, but I kept calling the meetings, and we all got to know each other better, on another level. I kept stressing that we were a team, that we needed to be friends, even proud of each other—not just on the court, but in school and elsewhere. A teammate is a special person, and even if we didn't like the person, we needed to get past it. I think it eventually worked.

Boys have the same problem, but for a different reason. They don't want anyone else to look better than them on the court, so it's about status—who is king of the hill! The approach to addressing this issue is different: more one on one. But the result—team work—is the same.

02

BASKETBALL POSITIONS

Generally in basketball, the taller players play underneath the hoop or along the baseline, at the center or forward positions, and shorter players fill the guard positions, where speed and agility are more important. There are usually one center, two forwards, and two guards on the floor. Forwards are sometimes called power forwards or shooting forwards, depending on whether they are generally called upon, in the plays selected by the coach, to play close to the hoop (the former) or to shoot from the corner (the latter).

Guards are also categorized. A point guard is known more for ballhandling and playmaking. Point guards get their name because they dribble the ball upcourt to the point area. It is from this area that point guards initiate offensive plays. The second guard is usually called a shooting guard or an off guard because he is located off the point in the wing area depicted in figure 2-1. The off guard is usually the team's best outside shooter, and plays are designed to get him an open shot from his wing position. He is also called upon to be an outlet guard—the person to whom a player underneath passes the ball after a rebound. Nowadays, more teams tend to get away from traditional designations, using numbers or floor positions to designate players. The number are usually: 1 = point guard, 2 = shooting guard, 3 = small forward, 4 = power forward, and 5 = center. The use of numbers or floor positions is further covered in chapter six when I discuss playmaking. For now, let's discuss each position.

THE CENTER

The tallest kid on your team will usually play at the center position, and he will usually be the focal point of the offense. His court area is mainly in the paint (or the lane), the area under the hoop between the free-throw lines.

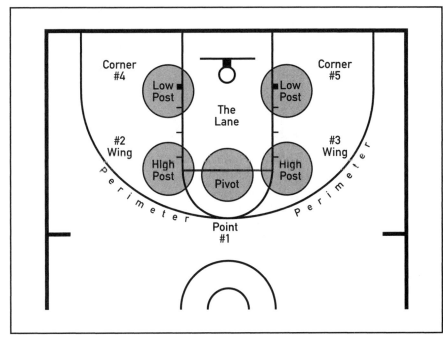

Floor-position names vary a bit around the country. Many coaches use numbers, rather than terms. The main floor positions are the corners, wings, low and high posts, and the point. The lane is the area between the foul lines.

CENTER ON OFFENSE

The main job of the center on offense is to get open for the pass underneath, that is, in the paint, and take the high-percentage jump shot, lay-up, or hook shot. The center must be able to catch quick passes! A center also tries to pick off or screen defenders by using his body to block a defender's path, freeing a teammate to drive for a shot. Finally, a center looks for rebounds, particularly offensive rebounds, and tries to score with them.

Post Positions. The majority of a center's actions occur at a post position. Posting up is a move in which the center straddles the side of the lane, facing the passer, looking for a pass underneath the basket. Up by the free-throw line, this position is called a high post. Closer to the basket, by the large lane block, it is called a low post. Remember that, when posting up, the player's foot cannot be inside the lane for more than three seconds, or the player will receive a violation. These violations drive coaches crazy. It's okay for a center to slide in and out of a post position to avoid the violation.

15

2-2. THE CENTER

Primary job of the center is to score from underneath with power moves.

Shots. A low-post position sets up a center to shoot near the hoop. A high-post position is used by the center for play-making, picks, give and go's, and many other plays discussed more fully in chapter six.

Centers at all levels of basketball must develop a workable hook shot, and they should try to learn to shoot left-handed from underneath. These shots are covered in chapter three. If your player is tall, make him practice mostly underneath the hoop, in the paint. Sure, he should practice outside shots. They are part of the game, and he will need them to be a fully rounded player. However, such practice should be mainly on his own. Unless he has a great outside shot, the team will need him underneath.

In your coaching, emphasize short jump shots, lay-ups, hook shots using both hands, fakes, fake pumps, tap-ins, pivot steps—all with minimal dribbling. These are skills, found in chapter three, that your center will need to perfect.

Posting Up. I'll have more to say about posting up in chapter six, since a center often posts up in offensive plays. Suffice it to say for now that, on offense, your center's most effective weapon is the post-up. In this position, the center stands underneath close to the hoop, straddling the foul line near the first block and facing the ball, with her back to the hoop and the defender. She stretches her arms out for a pass, leaning slightly back into and making contact with the defender. Underneath the hoop, players without the ball are usually allowed to make soft contact, such as when they are jockeying for position or leaning into each other, but they cannot push, shove, or bump each other. The post up effectively screens the defender from stealing a pass and allows the center

16

to "make a move" on the defender, that is, a quick maneuver to get a shot off. Posting-up is particularly effective when the center is taller and stronger than the defender.

The steps for posting up are:

1. The center heads to the low post, the area by the large block next to the foul line under the hoop area.

2. Through his positioning, he feels the defender on his posterior and keeps the other player in between his elbows, using his own elbows and inside hand to feel the defender, even to control him a bit. Coaches generally teach the center to "sit on the defenders thigh," since the defender will often try to push the center away from the hoop with his thigh. The center's target hand is out to show where he wants the pass, and other hand is back "feeling" the defender. When the center receives the pass, he quickly brings the ball in and holds it up under his chin, with his elbows out.

3. The center, or post player, makes himself feel wide, with his legs spread and his knees bent a bit. He tries to work his way backward without fouling. If the defender is directly behind the center, the center fakes a move to one side in order to move the defender to that side. The center keeps his back side in contact with the defender, so he knows which way to move.

4. Once the defender moves a bit to one side, the center holds the ball chin high and moves hard to the other side, drops the foot on that side back and in towards the hoop, and pivots on it around the defender as if he were a *post*, and then explodes upward. Depending on how close he is to the hoop, the player can take a power dribble, which allows for a two-footed jump. He shouldn't throw an elbow but should keep it out for protection and to pick up a possible foul. The center employs body fakes and shot fakes as needed. (See figure 2-3 on page 18.)

5. If no move to the hoop is available, centers should pass the ball back out. Centers need to know that they have to decide whether to make a move to the hoop or pass to someone else. You want your centers to think about scoring, but they shouldn't become a "black hole" from which nothing ever returns. They should be team players.

The Head-and-Shoulder Fake From Post Position. Post play is an attempt to score from underneath, and, as suggested above, it is much easier if an effective fake is part of the move. Perhaps the best move a center can make out of a low post is to head and shoulder fake to one side, then drop-step quickly the other way, pivot, and go up with strength. A

2-3. POSTING UP

Step 1: To post up—an effective way to set up a pass reception and a shot—the player keeps the defender "in the elbows," give target with hand away from defender, feel defender with arm closer to her, and back up as the ball is about to be passed. Player should "sit" on the defender's thigh if she tries to push you with her thigh.

Step 2: Fake to one side, keeping the feet stationary.

Step 3: Drop step with the right foot, then pushes off the left foot and quickly spins clockwise.

Step 4: Turns, take a hook shot. Posting up can be done on either side of the lane.

18

drop step is simply a step back toward the hoop with the inside foot (the foot farthest from the defender), followed by a spin for the shot. This move anticipates that the defender will initially go with the first fake, at least a bit. It is essentially a pivot backward and a shot off the dropped foot. Of course, if the defender is already to one side, then no fake is needed and the center just drop-steps with the other foot. The drop step can be used on either side of the lane, and it can be used for an inside or an outside pivot. The fake is most effective if the center can pivot either way, so the defender can't just close off one lane.

Practicing Moves

Given all of the above, it makes sense for your center to focus on and regularly practice all the moves which can be made from the post position.

The most common post move is for the player to fake right and move left (from a post on the right side of the lane) for a lay-up, a hook shot, or a fading short jump shot. (See the information on shooting in chapter two.) To be able to set up the move, the center needs to practice the footwork required to fake right/go left or fake left/go right. Remember, big players use power from the post position, and smaller players must rely more on speed, positioning, and fakes. Your players should practice accordingly. It's important for a young center to walk through and practice the footwork many, many times. Have him practice first without a defender until he is very comfortable with the drop-step.

A common bad habit of centers is the natural tendency to put the ball down or dribble it underneath. The pivot step is usually enough to let them cover whatever distance is needed out of a low post. Sure, there are times a single dribble is needed to punctuate a fake or to get closer to the hoop, but more often than not, the need for the dribble is just a failure to use the pivot step properly. Dribbling underneath is an invitation to have the ball stolen or bobbled in what is usually a very heavy traffic area.

It's helpful for a coach or parent to play a budding center one-on-one from the post position. It's great experience for everyone.

CENTER ON DEFENSE

On defense, the center must try to dominate the paint area and keep the opponents from shooting the high-percentage underneath shots. This involves fronting—getting the body or a hand in front of an opponent who is trying to post-up underneath—to prevent his getting a pass underneath. I'll discuss this further in chapter seven. This defense also involves blocking shots and otherwise harassing anyone venturing into the paint area. Underneath the hoop is the center's turf, and he needs to take charge of it.

Centers usually pick up a lot of fouls playing defense, particularly at young ages. This is because there is a lot of action and traffic underneath and also because of the players' inexperience. Blocking shots takes height or leaping ability because the ball should be blocked far enough from the shooter to avoid a foul. The preferred technique is to block across the ball, or straight up, but *not* toward the shooter, to minimize the chance of a foul. Whenever two kids go up very close to each other, chances are there will be some body contact. If the center is moving, or off the ground, and any body contact is made, a foul will usually be called. So a center must know that, unless she can dominate the shooter, the best technique underneath is just to stand still with arms raised straight up, trying to put some pressure on the shot or even draw an offensive foul. If the defender is still and contact is made, it's an offensive foul or charge. The best defense against a player driving for a lay-up is to establish position in front of that player, stay still, and take the offensive charge.

Rebounding. Perhaps the most important defensive responsibility of the center is to get rebounds. If the other team gets the rebound, it's an easy shot and two points. Therefore, it's essential for a defending center to get rebounds. This shouldn't be difficult, since defenders are usually positioned between their opponents and the hoop and should already be better positioned for the rebound.

2-4. DEFENSE UNDERNEATH

If a player is close to the shooter, fouls are commonly called. Stretch straight up and hold ground, hands straight up.

Boxing Out an Opponent. A key defensive strategy is to box out the opponent as he takes a shot. For the center, this skill is critical. When an opponent releases a shot, the center hesitates a second before turning to face the hoop for the rebound. This hesitation allows the center to see in which direction the opponent is going to get to the rebound. Then the center steps in the opponent's way, and, after blocking off the opponent, quickly turns around, sticks her posterior into the opponent, and stretches her arms sideways to make it tough for the opposing player to get around her, thereby making herself wide. Once the center gets the rebound, she looks to the sideline for a teammate, usually a guard, designated as the outlet and passes to her. We'll discuss this more in chapter seven.

POSITION DRILLS FOR CENTERS

Team drills will be presented in chapters six and seven, but I'll include a few here designed to improve the critical skills needed by centers—shooting underneath and posting up. Other drills on skills such as boxing out and rebounding will be presented with team drills, since they apply to most positions. These are drills that centers can do on their own, or with a friend or helpful parent, to focus on their specialty.

2-5. **BOXING OUT**

Boxing out an offensive player is an effective way to get rebounds. These two defenders demonstrate great box-out positions because their bodies are low and wide, and they make contact with the opponent.

Rapid-Shooting Drill. The center stands under the hoop, trying to make as many short shots as possible in one minute. Count the shots made. The objective of the drill is to increase quickness in power leaping under time pressure. Over time, the center should try to increase the number of successful shots in a minute. Keep tabs of the player's prior personal record.

Medley-Shooting Drill. The center is underneath the hoop and shoots a medley of shots, such as righty jumper, lefty jumper, righty hook, lefty hook, fake and shoot jumper, and double pump jumper. Missed shots get tapped in. Encourage the center to try and get a whole medley without a miss, then go for two times through without a miss.

Post-it Drill. The center runs across the lane to the low post, and the coach or parent passes. The center jump-stops to catch the ball and drop-steps to shoot. After a while, have the player add in a fake to one side and then a drop step to the other. He should practice drop-stepping to both sides. After he gets the move down, add defensive pressure to the drill.

THE FORWARD

Forwards are also taller players, usually the next tallest after the center. They need to be tall because, like the center, they are frequently called upon to play underneath the hoop. However, forwards also cover the wing area and especially cover the corners of the court, so they need to develop an outside shot, preferably from the corner, and they must be able to dribble and pass.

Every position on the team requires some skills unique to that position: For small forwards, these are the corner shot and the baseline drive. The power, or weak-side, forwards need to be able to get an offensive rebound, since the shot will often come from the opposite side of the court and will thus bounce toward them. Of course, forwards need to be complete players and need to develop all skills of the game, particularly those of the center, but you should emphasize and practice the skills most specifically required of the forward. This is where the parent can be most helpful, assisting in the practice of those special skills. Forwards spend a lot of time in the corner or baseline area, and they need to perfect their skills from that location and perspective.

FORWARD ON OFFENSE

On offense, the first duty of the forward is to follow the steps required in offensive pattern plays, as covered in chapter six. These plays are usually designed to get the forward free for a pass into the corner area or to have her pick a defender to free up a teammate. Most teams will have a series of plays, or a normal offensive routine, requiring the forward to catch a pass or screen for another player.

Key Move for the Forward. Your forward needs to develop a move that frees him up for a pass. The best move, the corner jab or v-jab, has the forward make a fake dash to the hoop, take two quick steps toward the center, then quickly plant his foot and dart back to the corner for the pass. The idea behind any fake is for a player to *relate* to the defender, try to feel he is actually pulling the defender to one side. Once the defender commits to following the fake, the forward darts back the other way. (See figure 2-6.) Another move is the opposite, often called the two-step: The forward takes two strong steps toward the corner and then quickly reverses back toward the hoop for a pass.

Handling the Ball. When the forward gets the ball, she simply follows the offensive routine. Usually someone moves to the hoop for a possible pass or the center posts-up low for a pass. Someone may come out to block, or pick, the defender guarding the forward, freeing her up to drive to the hoop. Screens and picks, perhaps the most important of offensive concepts, are covered in chapter six. Otherwise, the forward may need to make her own way, fake outside and drive the baseline or jab-step and take a jump shot. If all else fails, she should pass the ball back out to the wing and start another offensive series.

Because forwards often get the ball in the corner, too far away to shoot, they need to be able to pass the ball effectively. Different types of passes are covered in chapter four.

Forwards are sometimes called upon to play under the hoop, so the forward should practice all offensive and defensive skills mentioned for centers—posting, hook shots, boxing out, fronting a player, avoiding fouls, taking charges, and rebounding.

Defending the Baseline Drive. Unique to the forward position on defense is the need to prevent the baseline drive. Forwards never want an opponent to successfully drive inside, that is, get between them and the baseline. If that occurs, the likelihood of a score by the opponents increases dramatically. Forwards should always close off the baseline drive with the leg closest to the baseline. Their teammates can help in the other direction.

Defending the Fake Shot and Drive. The forward also needs to defend against the fake shot and drive. Because there is a strong natural tendency to try to block outside shots, the fake shot and drive is usually very successful, even at younger ages. We'll discuss this all in more detail when we discuss defense in chapter seven. We'll also talk about how to defend against the outside shot.

2-6. CORNER JAB OR TWO-STEP

Step 1: The corner takes two sharp steps inside to get the defender in motion.

Step 2: Plant the second foot a hard push back.

Step 3: Quickly dart back to the corner for the pass.

DRILLS FOR FORWARDS

As noted earlier, team drills will be presented in later chapters, but I'll include a few here designed to improve the critical skills needed by forwards. Those skills are corner moves and shots, baseline work, and offensive rebounding. Other drills on skills such as boxing out and defensive rebounding, as well as screening, will be presented with team drills, since they apply to most positions. These are drill that forwards can do on their own, or with a friend or helpful parent, to focus on their specialty.

Jabbing and Two-Stepping Drill. The forward stands in corner area, closely defended. Someone in the point-guard position readies to pass. The forward tries jab steps and two steps to get free for a pass; the defender tries to steal.

Corner-Shots Drill. The coach or parent feeds the player jump shots from corner area. The distance is close enough to be in the shooter's range, gradually extending over time as accuracy increases. Twenty-five shots per session; shots should be made quickly with a reasonable jump, and the coach or parent should look for good form.

Baseline-Drive Drill. The forwards line up along the baseline and jab-step, catch a pass from a coach or guard, fake the shot or fake drive towards the high post, and then take the baseline in for a lay-up.

THE GUARD

There is plenty of room for shorter players in the game of basketball. Guards are usually the shortest players on the team. However, keep in mind that in the pros, the guards are often about 6'4". It's all relative. The biggest guys (the seven footers) are usually found underneath. In 1988, I enjoyed watching Trenton State College games. A friend's son played on the team, and they had a good shot at the Division III National Championship. The team also had a 5'6" guard named Greg Grant who eventually broke the all-time national scoring record for collegiate careers with over 2,600 points and went on to play pro ball. Greg was the ultimate guard and a wonder to behold on the court.

TYPES OF GUARDS

The Point Guard

The point guard is like a quarterback on a football team. After the ball comes to front-court, she positions herself at the top of the key—the point of the free throw circle farthest from the basket—and starts the offensive play. A point guard needs to be able to shoot outside, drive inside, and pass with snappy effectiveness. Although shooting skills are not as important for a point guard as dribbling and passing, shooting ability always helps. Usually, if your team has one good outside shooter, that's all you really need, and the shooting guard needs to be positioned in the wing, close to the hoop.

If a player shows promise with the outside shot, urge her to practice on her own to increase her accuracy.

Point guards should be encouraged to be leaders. They are to communicate constantly with the team, helping others move to where they are needed. They call the play, take the inbound pass, and urge teammates to hustle, keep hands up, and be aggressive. The guard's primary responsibility is to be the first line of defense, and so the point must ensure that she is prepared for the transition to defense.

The point guard also calls the offensive plays, usually with fingers or a raised fist.

The Shooting Guard

A shooting guard is also called an off guard or a two guard and usually plays the wing area, between the point and the forward areas. He may have a favorite spot where he shoots the best and where he will hang out. This player needs to shoot with accuracy and to be able to pass effectively. The shooting guard will often have his defender picked or screened, and so he needs to use the pick or screen effectively. When a play breaks down, the shooting guard is a pivotal position, and he is often the one expected to *make something happen*—to drive, shoot, lay off a pass to the center, or kick out a pass to a forward.

Dribbling. Dribbling is the most important skill in basketball; without it, the team will never get to shoot. I'll spend a whole chapter on this skill. A guard needs to be able to dribble effectively with either hand. She needs to be able to take a defender one-on-one and dribble around him. She needs to be able to dribble in close quarters and heavy traffic and to speed dribble at a dead run. (See figure 2-7.) The kid on the team who can dribble the best should bring the ball up the floor. If a team doesn't have a guard who can get the ball down the court, it will fail miserably. For players at young ages, local rules usually require the defense to wait until the ball crosses mid-court before attacking. This is a welcome rule because without it, few balls would pass mid-court.

You must emphasize dribbling in team and personal practice. Your guards can practice anywhere because they don't need a basketball court to dribble. Since dribbling is the most essential skill in basketball, your players should practice dribbling one-on-one. A guard should dribble while another player tries to steal the ball. Dribbling under pressure is the best possible practice.

Passing. Next in importance to dribbling. Guards need to be able to pass the ball deceptively, accurately, and with strength and speed on the ball. (See chapter five.) In general, your guards should know where their teammates are, dribble with their heads

2-7. SPEED DRIBBLE

The heart of youth basketball, particularly at very young ages, is the ability of guards to get the ball safely to the offense.

up and eyes scanning the play, and spot the open teammate. The best technique for the guard is to pass on the dribble, to never stop dribbling. The kid who does these best should be your point guard.

Floor Vision. The guard needs to know where each teammate is and who is free for a pass. Of course, at intermediate and advanced levels, the play is more choreographed with specific offensive play patterns (chapter six), but guards need to try to see the whole floor. It's not enough to see one player or groups of two to three players; the guard's awareness must include all ten players. This is floor vision. Some kids have it more naturally, but the concept needs to be repeated constantly by the coach in practice scrimmages. Floor vision is as much a state of mind as a skill, and it certainly needs be practiced. When a guard gets a ball, he should square up, head up, and, if not under too much pressure, try to quickly gaze at the whole court and take it all in. This quick look will help the guard decide the direction of a pass or dribble. Of course, floor vision is most possible when dribbling skills are superior, so the guard can concentrate on the movement of others instead of just his own defender. So, while his primary duty will be to run the offense, a guard with good floor vision will spot the open player, or better yet, the player about to become open, and thus pass for a high-percentage shot.

GUARDS ON DEFENSE

Defensive guards need to steal passes. A kid who can steal passes is very valuable because a stolen pass usually leads to an easy score. Chapter seven deals with this skill in more detail. Defensive guards pressure the outside shooter and, more importantly, ensure that the ball carrier doesn't drive by them. Stress to your guards that the key to good defense is preventing penetration to the basket and keeping the opponent away from the high-percentage shots.

Another key defensive skill is to play the transition. Guards need to remember that they are the first line of defense to a steal or a fast break by the other team. It's important not to be caught out of place during the transition to defense. Guards must catch up to the ball and slow things down, forcing the ball wide to allow their teammates time to get back.

DRILLS FOR GUARDS

As noted for the other positions, team drills generally will be presented in chapters six and seven, but I'll include a few here designed to specifically reference critical skills needed by guards. Those skills are dribbling and floor vision. For shooting guards, well … the most important skill is shooting from a favorite spot.

Sprint-Dribble Drill. The guard dribbles the full length of the court, timed with a stopwatch. The ball must be under control. Do this drill five times. Take the best time, and have the guard try to beat it the next time. Let the team know the record, and even the all-time record, from former teams.

Floor-Visioning Drill. Two coaches or players stand in the corners. The guard starts at the top of the key in backcourt and dribbles the ball under pressure. The coaches alternate quickly raising their hands, and the point guard must call out the coach's name that raised his hand as soon as it goes up. This forces the guard to see the corners while dribbling under pressure.

Wing-Shots Drill. The coach, a player, or parent stands in the point area and feeds passes to the shooting guard. The guard should be positioned in the wing area, close enough to be in the shooter's range, gradually extending this distance over time as accuracy increases. The guard may move around a bit, but this drill is designed to have him shoot from his favorite spot, thus increasing shooting accuracy. Have the guard take twenty-five shots per session; shots should be made quickly with a reasonable jump, and the coach should look for good form.

SHOOTING

Shooting is fun. It's the glory of basketball. I'll never forget the smiles that broke across the faces of kids as they made their first basket ever in a game. It was a rite of passage.

A kid who can consistently hit shots, especially jump shots, is a rare and valuable player. Teams often build their offense around their best shooter by running plays that get this player free for a good shot. Kids know who can shoot the ball. Coaches know, too. If a kid can shoot, he's told to go for it. If a kid can't consistently make a certain shot, he's told not to take the shot. This is certainly true by high school and will also be true for the more competitive grade-school traveling teams. At beginner and intermediate levels of course, where learning is or should be the only goal, players will be encouraged to take all open shots.

The greatest shooters make 70 to 80 percent of close shots or free throws, nearly 50 percent of jump shots, and maybe a third of their three-point shots, in game conditions. If your player wants to be a shooter, he must develop a shot he can make consistently in practice. It makes sense.

It is not essential to be a good shooter, but if a kid can't shoot, he will need to be very good at dribbling and passing or rebounding. Role players such as these are important, too! Most kids will not become great shooters, so it's important for them to develop the other skills.

TYPES OF SHOOTERS

There are outside shooters and inside shooters. A good outside shooter is someone who can sink about half of their shots from twelve feet or farther. They are the chosen people of basketball. A winning team almost always has a good outside shooter. I played in a youth league as a kid, and we had a great shooter named Rich. He scored twenty points a game and led us to a championship. It was great to know he was on the court and would stick the ball when things got close!

Everyone on the team must be a decent inside shooter. An open shot from underneath is very high-percentage, and the offensive plays usually try to get the ball to an open, big player underneath. Tall players will obviously be expected to take most inside shots, but everyone needs to be able to deliver two points from underneath most of the time. An inside shot, also called a lay-up because it's taken close and expected to go in, actually requires a degree of feel and touch because it is banked off the backboard or soft-touched gently over the rim. A player must know how hard and where to bounce the ball off the backboard. Young kids often bank it too hard, and the ball bounces away off the rim.

SHOOTING CAN BE LEARNED: 10,000 SHOTS!

The good news is that shooting can be learned. Sure, naturally talented kids will learn a lot faster and shoot with a higher percentage, but all kids can learn to shoot. It takes many thousands of shots to significantly raise a shooter's percentage, but, remember, it really doesn't take that long to shoot a thousand shots.

The best way to teach shooting is simply to help a kid shoot ten thousand shots. In 1984, I had a great experience with my older son, Jack, which was the most memorable coaching experience of my life. I mentioned it in the preface, but it bears repeating here. I think it's a great testimony to what an individual parent can do, and it may be the best story I can leave you with in this book.

Jack was entering his junior year in high school. He had played basketball, but for a number of reasons, including injuries, he had not gotten a lot of playing time or experience.

Jack was tall and quick and very much wanted to be able to contribute more during his final two high-school years. He and I discussed it, and we agreed that we would spend that summer in an intensive program.

We spent hours every day during the summer working on skills. I would stand under the hoop and rapidly feed Jack rebounds for short jump shots. He shot and shot until his arms nearly fell off. He would dribble, shoot fouls, and play one-on-one against me. By the time we were done, he couldn't miss short jump shots. His school coach told me he had never seen such improvement, and Jack eventually broke into the starting lineup. This is a boy who was cut as a freshman!

The experience taught me how much difference a parent can make in helping a child improve, especially when the child is motivated.

You need to be patient with young kids because they develop shots at different paces. I coached a clinic for eight- and nine-year-olds a few years ago. A boy named Eric was one of the most talented athletes in the group, but he was so full of energy that he couldn't make a basket. He just banged the ball hard off the backboard. When Eric was twelve, I saw him play on my son's school team. He was still rough, but you could see the beginnings of gracefulness. The boy became a very good player; for him, as for many kids, it just takes time and perseverance.

Perhaps the greatest contribution a coach or parent can make is to help a player get beyond the frustrating experience of being a beginner. Help her hang in there! Feed them 10,000 shots! Then start over!

ABOUT OUTSIDE SHOOTING

The introduction of the three-point shot, a long shot of over nineteen feet, has restored outside shooting to basketball at the high-school and college levels. At youth levels, most kids can't shoot that far. However, it brings a needed dimension back to the game, and gives shorter players a chance to develop a skill that will give them more playing time.

In practice, give your kids a chance to show what they have. In games at beginner or recreational levels, urge them to shoot whenever they have an open shot. But stress to them that an outside shot, in particular, is difficult to develop during team practice. A player must do that on his own time. It takes ten thousand shots to even begin to have a decent shot! My younger son played with a boy named Matt who spent hours nearly every day, even in the rain, shooting jump shots in his driveway. Because of this practice, the boy could shoot, and he was always allowed, even expected, to take the outside shot. It's a privilege which must be earned. At more advanced levels, players will be allowed to shoot from a distance at which they can make a shot at least half the time.

We'll cover offensive playmaking in chapter six. Suffice it to say that a play is a series of movements designed to free up a shooter, usually by screening or picking off the player who is defending her. If the play works, a shooter is open to take a high-percentage shot. High-percentage shots are mainly shots within the player's range, which are taken with a minimum of defensive pressure, thus allowing the shooter to use good shooting form.

KNOW YOUR RANGE AND SHOOT CONFIDENTLY WITHIN IT

I'm not being negative when I tell kids to "know your range." Basketball is a team game. If a player at advanced levels, certainly by high school, hasn't spent the hours needed to shoot fifteen- to nineteen-foot shots, he can't develop such a shot during games. There is no individual right to shoot long shots.

Most players can and should take shots of ten feet or less, if they can get the shot off without being blocked; but only players who have earned the long ones should ordinarily take them. I never say never, because there are times everyone should shoot a long shot, particularly when players underneath have strong rebounding position.

A player learns through practice the range within which he makes most of his shots. Then there is a gray area, usually ten to fifteen feet. Finally, there is a range in which he misses most shots.

When a player is within his effective range, he should be confident enough to take a good shot whenever he can. How often do we see a player refuse to take a simple eight-foot jumper because he lacks the confidence? Players should be encouraged to shoot those shots—even poor shooters will make a lot of the shorter ones. A player must expect the ball to go in the hoop when shooting within his range.

Of course, the best remedy for lack of confidence is simply more practice. As a coach, you will use practice time mostly for teaching general dynamics and for conditioning. Often, because of time constraints, shooting practice gets little time. You can tell the kids how to shoot, and some shooting time should be built into the practice plan, particularly to ensure good form, as discussed in chapter eight. However, you should urge them to practice on their own and with their parents. Kids who practice will get more playing time because they will put numbers up on the scoreboard. Coaches keep statistics, such as number of points, rebounds, steals, assists, turnovers—they all count! The kids with the numbers will play. Some coaches don't know talent if they fall over it, but the numbers usually don't lie, and lineups are often based on the numbers.

DON'T FORCE SHOTS

While players need to seek and take high-percentage shots, the worst shot is one that is forced. When under extreme pressure, off balance, or far out of range, a player should not take a shot. (Forced shots are usually met with a quick move to the bench.) Instead, a player should pass the ball and continue to search for a high-percentage shot. Again, this varies with the level of play. Beginners are urged to take any shot they can within ten feet of the hoop. Shots at this level are hard to come by. After a few years of experience, though, coaches and players should start talking about high-percentage shots and about avoiding the forced shot.

Look for the Open Player Underneath

An outside shooter may be good, but she'll never shoot more accurately than a player underneath the hoop. Also, remember that a faked shot is a great decoy and a good opportunity to pass to the big players underneath. A good team player always looks for an open player with a better shot. That's how ball games are won—good percentage shooting.

Keep All Options Open

When a player fakes, the idea isn't for him to just fake a dribble in order to shoot or fake a shot in order to dribble; he should do what the situation calls for. If the opponent takes the fake dribble, he should shoot. Sometimes, a player has to try several fakes before he can capitalize on the one that works best. I discussed earlier the concept of relating to feeling the defender's balance, trying to *pull* the defender in a direction. Once the defender is off balance, your player should go the other way.

THE TOP TEN FUNDAMENTALS OF OUTSIDE SHOOTING

I've already covered some of the advantages of outside shooting. Now let's discuss the mechanics.

1. Relaxed Confidence. Ya Gotta Believe! I'm going to harp on this point, but good shooters make baskets *because they know they can shoot!* They've shot tens of thousands of baskets, and they simply are sure of their shot and expect the ball to go into the basket. They either have an innately accurate shot or they have developed a great shot. When a player is relaxed and confident, she will naturally resort to proper form, balance, and focus. It all just *clicks* for her.

2. Square to the Basket in the Triple-Threat Stance. The triple-threat stance is a multipurpose position from which the player can shoot, dribble, pass, or fake in any direction. The weight is forward on the balls of the feet. The feet are balanced under the shoulders and pointed toward the basket. The knees and waist are bent, ready to move in any direction; head and shoulders are square and level; head and chin are up; the ball is up in front of the chest; elbows are out to protect it. (See figure 3-1.) The hands are open, fingers lightly spread, thumb tips slightly separated on the ball, a position from which the player can pass or shoot. The key, when a shot is contemplated, is for the shoulders, hips, and feet to be squared towards the basket. Many great shooters will open the stance a bit, and my feeling is that coaches should teach kids to square but allow for a bit of openness if they are more comfortable with it. I'll cover the triple-threat stance again in the chapters on offensive and defensive dynamics.

3. Fakes Make Space; One-on-One Moves. A fake or feint is a valuable move used by a closely defended shooter to throw the defender off balance and to open up an unobstructed shot or to open a lane to the hoop. Usually, a faked dribble or jab step

33

The triple-threat stance requires that the player's weight is forward on the balls of the feet, knees and waist are bent, head is up, shoulders are square, and the ball is held up by the chest.

will get a young defender to move to the side or to back up a bit. As soon as the shooter gets the ball, she jab-steps strongly and directly toward the defender. Sometimes a short jab followed by a full jab with the same foot does the trick. When the defender reacts and takes a step back, the shooter takes the shot.

Another great fake move is to raise the ball high very quickly as if to shoot, even looking at the hoop. This causes the defender to come forward and allows the ball handler to dribble past him. A combination of jab steps and fake shots often creates a good scoring opportunity and should be automatic whenever a player, especially a guard, gets the ball. (See again figure 2-6.)

You can't overemphasize to your players the importance of fakes. If a defensive player gets a distracting hand up in your shooter's face, his shooting percentage drops considerably. A good tip for players is to try to *feel* the defender's balance. The player tries to mentally push the defender off-balance into one direction or the other, and he can almost feel when the defender leans one way or the other. When he tries to relate to the defender's balance, the fake is more convincing. The defender must believe that the shooter is going to dribble. Have your players practice this by working in pairs, faking each other.

Fake-Away Drill. A good drill for the concept of fakes is to place two cones seven to nine feet apart and have two players face each other. The offensive player (without a ball) fakes and jabs and tries to get around the defender (who slide steps to cut him off). Vary the cones to make it challenging. This drill give the players a sense of what a good fake can do and also helps them to learn defense against a fake. At some time, introduce a ball into the drill, but don't let the defender use her hands.

4. Shoot from the Legs; Jump High and Straight Up. The power for a jump shot comes from the legs and hips. The hands guide the shot and transfer power from the legs. The highest percentage jump shot is straight up. A straight jump gets the ball higher and over the tips of the defender's fingers, which reduces the odds that the shot will be blocked.

Players sometimes lean to one side as they jump, which results in a slight ball motion to that direction. Sure, defensive pressure forces a shooter to lean, or fade away (lean backward), and sometimes (not often) a player can perfect such a shot. But the higher percentage is always straight up, thus ensuring that the shooter does not have to calculate and compensate for body lean. Teach your players to jump as high and as gracefully as possible, to involve both feet, and to spring off the toes. Players should practice feeling the balance in their feet before jumping. The player

3–2. JUMP STRAIGHT UP

The highest percentage shots, that is, those that are successful most often, are made with the body straight, not learning toward the hoop.

35

releases the ball before the peak of the jump, which assures that the force of the legs get into the shot. Stress to your team that shooting starts in the legs and lower body. Talk about the lazy jump shot, an overly relaxed shot without significant height in the jump. Such a shot can be more easily blocked and is less accurate and intense. Using both feet adds to the balance and control of the jump, thus improving the odds for a goal.

5. Cradle High. For an outside shot, the hands form a cradle for the ball, which is held high, in front of and a bit higher than the eyes, to minimize the chances of a blocked shot. This allows the player to see the basket from underneath the ball, between the arms.

At first, kids don't have the strength to shoot from a high cradle, and so they "set" the ball just below their line of sight and push it out with two hands. One-handed shots more than ten feet out are very tough until maybe fifth or sixth grade. One handed foul shots, fifteen feet away, may be possible by sixth grade. Yet, it is important for even beginners to learn the one-handed shot, even if it's just from a few feet out. Teach it the right way, and let them work it out.

The ball is cradled in the shooting hand, sitting on comfortably spread fingers and the upper palm. Feet are square, the shooting foot perhaps a bit in front of the other foot, pointed at the hoop. The ball is raised and rotated a bit so the shooting hand is behind and a bit lower than the ball, the arm close to the body and bent at the elbow. The non-shooting hand should slide a bit until it's straight up on the opposite side. It gently holds the ball into the cradle so that the player is in control of the ball but not squeezing it. The non-shooting hand is neutral; it adds nothing to the shot.

Kids often shoot with two hands, since they are not strong enough to shoot with one. However, they must understand that one-handed shots are higher-percentage shots. As they get stronger, players need to make the transition from a two-handed shot to a one-handed shot, and they will often add a little push with the non-shooting hand. This is a very common but important problem with shooting form. Look for it, and teach your players to change this habit. It's a matter of awareness, and so you need to harp on it for a while.

The player's hands should be soft, handling the ball like a fragile egg on a launching pad. The ball rests mainly on the fingers and upper section of the palm, with not much more than incidental contact with the base of the palm, especially the heel. The head and shoulders are level and square so that the body is balanced and erect.

3-3. CRADLE HIGH, SQUARE SHOULDERS, AND POINT ELBOWS

Shooting with the elbow angled outward, as shown by this player, is the most common flaw for beginners.

Here, the player's arm is kept parallel with the body, the elbow pointing toward the hoop. The hand cradles the ball slightly above the head, and the shoulders are square.

6. Foot and Hand and Elbow Point to the Hoop. The most important aspect of outside shooting is the position of the shooting hand and elbow, which must aim toward the basket. Kids often point that elbow outward. Have them keep the elbow in, not uncomfortably squeezed in as some coaches try to get them to do, but fairly straight. More than anything else, even more than a body lean, an outward elbow will send a ball in an errant direction and will prevent the wrist from properly launching the ball. The upper part of the shooting arm should be, generally, parallel to the floor, and it must always point in the direction of the basket.

At the top of the jump, with the shooting cradle raised straight up and extended, the player flicks the wrist, placing a 30-degree spin on the ball with the thumb side of the hand. Only one hand shoots; the other is passive and simply falls away. The player shoots just before the top of the jump, again to avoid the defender's outstretched hands and to ensure that some of the jump's strength is transferred to the ball. A shot begins in the legs, and the power is transferred to the ball. The shooting hand must be relaxed, and the release must be consistant with each shot, the power coming from the legs to reach the hoop.

Wall Drill. The best way to develop good form is to shoot repeatedly against a wall. The wall delivers the ball directly back, so the player can take many practice shots.

Have your players pick a spot on the wall about ten-feet high and try to hit it on a downward arc. Study each hand, body position, wrist flick, cradle, arc, and toe point. Ensure that they get a good jump off the floor with each shot.

7. The Release: Gooseneck Wrist Flick. The gooseneck wrist flick is as important to shooting as is pointing the elbow at the hoop. Most kids develop all kinds of crazy hand techniques, such as closing the fingers into a fist as they shoot or coming down with the middle finger or the pinkie finger. This is a sign they are using their hands to give power to the ball, instead of the lower body doing the power work. The hand is just guide. The natural and correct form is to flick the ball out of the cradle by turning the palm down and out, shooting with the three inside fingers. The little finger stays in basically the same position, pointing elegantly upward, before and after the shot. The thumb and index finger, however, move forward, down, and out. The index finger does most of the work of shooting.

When the shooting hand turns down and out, this puts a reverse 30 degree-spin (from the vertical) on the ball. That's how you know the shot has been done properly.

3-4. THE GOOSENECK RELEASE

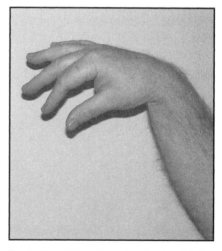

The final position of the shooting hand is the gooseneck.

Notice how, after the ball is flicked toward the hoop, the shooting hand holds the gooseneck position, while the other hand falls away from the ball.

38

The final position of the shooting hand is called a gooseneck. The best shooters seem to frame or freeze their release posture for a moment after shooting, so the gooseneck can be seen clearly. I don't urge players to freeze the release, other than to develop the gooseneck because you want them to react and follow the ball.

The left hand does not add any power on a right-handed shot. It passively cradles the ball and then merely falls away during the shot. The shooting hand does not snap back, but either gently follows-through on the shot in a downward arc or is held relatively stationary for a moment. Either style is okay.

Gooseneck Drill. If your player does not properly flick the ball from the cradle, she can remedy this problem with some drills, particularly if you catch it early enough. Perhaps the best way for the child to change form is to shoot repeatedly against a high wall and to go through a few hundred wrist flicks, concentrating only on the form of her hand movement, freezing it for a moment. A few such practice sessions will help make any correction needed. Good form is essential to shooting.

8. Aim Just Beyond the Point at the Front of the Rim. Concentration is essential to good shooting, and the goal is for the player to reduce any unnecessary movement and to be balanced and still. A shooter should aim to set the ball on or just beyond the front of the hoop. He should do this by focusing on the point of the hoop closest to him and setting the ball on top of that spot. This reduces the focus to a single point, instead of the whole space of the hoop. The shooter should mentally clear away anything else but the point on the front of the hoop. He tries to loft the ball and set it down just past the point of the hoop closest to him.

9. Arcing the Ball: Avoid Throwing Bricks. A sufficiently arced ball has the best chance of scoring because it drops through the largest possible hoop opening. A lot of players shoot bricks—balls that travel directly at the basket. These linear shots utilize a smaller window through the hoop than arced shots and, therefore, have less chance of scoring. Too high of an arc, however, is unnecessary and just complicates the shot. For a comfortable arc, a good rule of thumb is to peak the arc with the bottom of the ball at about three feet higher than the basket, on a fifteen-foot or more shot. In close, a one-and-a-half to two-foot arc is okay. (See figure 3-5.)

Often the defender will get a hand up in front of the shooter. Then the shooter must react to avoid being blocked. Sometimes it's enough for the player to give the ball a bit more arc, enough to get over the hand, or perhaps to go for a bank shot, which adds both arc and a slight change in direction. Another solution is for the shooter to double pump, that is, to withdraw the ball momentarily and restart the shot. Alternately, the

3–5. **SHOOTING ARC**

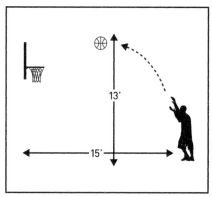

The proper arc is about two to three feet above the rim on a twelve to fifteen foot jump shot. A too-low arc is common in youth sports; such shots are called bricks.

player can fade away from the defender and lean back to get more shooting angle and arc. Players must react to the defender, relate to the defender, sense where she is at all times, and take what opportunities are given.

A common error in shooting is to shoot the ball too far, past the rim. If this happens, chances are the player's forearm is too involved in pushing the ball. Have her use more wrist and less forearm.

Arcing Drill. A good drill here is to get a twelve-foot pole and let kids see how their arc compares. If a player shoots a twelve-foot jump shot, the ball should clear the pole.

10. Follow the Shot. I think the toughest habit for a kid to break is that of standing immobile and watching the ball as it moves to the basket. A small but significant percentage of rebounds bounce back toward the shooter, and a player who moves to follow the shot to the basket will often get a rebound and a second chance. In shooting practice, tell the team to always take at least one or two steps forward following the shot, just to develop the habit. The habit of standing still and watching the ball is usually developed during shooting practice, and it's a bad one. Players should move to the hoop as they come down from the shot.

INSIDE SHOOTING—MECHANICS AND DYNAMICS

Basketball underneath the hoop is the tall person's turf. The highest-percentage shooting, 70 percent or better, comes inside, underneath the hoop, or within six feet or so. It's the boiler room area of the court, where you'll find a lot of grunting, leaning, boxing out, shot blocking, rebounding, fancy lay-ups, slam dunks, hook shots and soft-touch jumpers sometimes banked off the glass. It's the world of basketball at its best. Sure, the three-point shots have opened the game up, and a player with quick hands is valuable for dribbling and stealing passes, but the game is still most exciting in the paint, the area between the foul lines (usually painted in a different color). A big man in the paint should feel like a lion in his den ... on his turf!

It's rare for a player to be successful underneath without at least average or above-average height. Short, quick players can sometimes zip past the big men and get a shot off if they are agile. Such players can visit, but not live, underneath. Big players get rebounds, block shots, and score points under the hoop. If a player is short, it's not a problem, but he must learn to dribble, pass, and shoot outside. Guide him in the direction appropriate to his size.

There are basically three inside shots: the driving lay-up, the short jump shot (sometimes called a chippie), and the hook.

THE LAY-UP

A lay-up is still the most exciting shot in basketball, and it's also one of the simplest. Kids dream of Michael Jordan dribbling toward the basket, leaping and flying through the air, and spinning into a reverse slam dunk. My thirteen-year-old son regularly broke into his imaginary move in our hallway, dunking into an imaginary basket. Well, young kids won't dunk for a while, but a drive and lay-up are certainly possible and should be emphasized and perfected above all other forms of shooting.

The reason is simple. Outside shooting is tough. A kid has to shoot thousands of shots before she can consistently hit the hoop. No problem; it just takes time. However, lay-ups can be learned more quickly. The youngest kids usually play pretty poorly on defense, so an offensive player who can dribble a bit will be able to advance the ball up close for an inside shot. It looks good and will get a cheer from the fans. It will help the team, and your player will take a big step forward in development. Most importantly, it's easy to do and comes quickly with a little practice.

For young beginners, the scores are low. The players generally can't shoot outside (or inside). A kid who can drive a few steps to the hoop and shoot a lay-up will have the best chance of scoring in youth basketball. If you are a parent, teach your child to do lay-ups, and, more quickly than with any other skill, her confidence will grow and with it, the ball player within will emerge.

One of the themes in coaching should always be confidence building, and this certainly reflects my general approach to coaching. I believe it's good to get kids going, to focus on something they can use right away, sort of jump-start the engine. Once a kid gets

03

to a point where she can contribute to a team, confidence takes over. Kids on a team will pass the ball to a player if they feel she can do something with it; otherwise, they will tend to look for someone who can. This is why I emphasize lay-ups for beginner-level play.

Here are the basics of driving (dribbling) to the basket and shooting a lay-up. Make sure you focus the kids on the following information when they are shooting lay-ups. The shot is the most common in hoops and is used at all age levels, early in practice, and just before games. It's also a great warm-up.

1. Make a Move. A lay-up usually starts when the player gets the ball about ten to twenty feet from the basket. If it's a designed play, such as a screen, then the player receives the ball on the run and continues to the hoop. More often, however, a player gets a pass or rebound and needs to make an individual move, that is, fake the defender. I have talked about fakes before, so I won't repeat it all here. The idea is to get the defender off-balance, feint one way or fake a shot, and then drive around him going the opposite way from the fake.

2. Claim the Lane and Explode Through It. Once a lane for dribbling is available, the player very quickly claims it. He can't dribble through a stationary defender, but he can claim any open lane. I always say that a player should drive as close to the defender as possible. If the defender reacts and moves back into that lane, he will commit a foul. The official will usually call the foul on a moving defender. Encourage players to claim the lane and stick to it. It always helps to get the other team to foul: The idea is to pick a point just on the outside the defender's shoulder and drive your shoulder right by it. If the defender reaches in, he fouls. Otherwise, break to the hoop! Too often, kids in a lay-up line dribble in slowly, casually. Have them get the feeling of preparing for a powerful launch in the last few steps; get into the habit every time.

3. Keep Everything Low. Early in a driving lay-up, the player keeps shoulders down, elbows in, waist and knees bent, and head up, and dribbles the ball low to the floor. This helps quickness, increases ball control, and protects the ball. The player should take care not to bump the opponent or lower the shoulder into him. She should stay low and steady.

4. Take the Two Free Steps and Find an Opening. The last two steps of a shooting drive are the most important. They are free; that is, no dribble is required. (Actually, the first step comes off the last dribble and establishes the pivot; only one "free" step is technically allowed. Frankly, I can't figure out the Pro rules on this anymore; it seems that extra steps are okay as long as they look great!) These last two "giant" steps usually cover a fair bit of ground. Since your player is no longer dribbling, he has the opportunity to look up for an opening. The player holds the ball firmly in both hands and must know what the defender is doing, so he can avoid a block or a charge. Usually, a big player underneath the hoop will react once your player drives by the first defender, so everything must happen very quickly. The two giant steps are often enough to get the player to a spot where he can lay up the ball to the basket.

A great drill for making this point is to have a child start at the foul line and make a lay-up with only one dribble. It's easily done, and it teaches the player how much distance he can cover without much dribbling. After practicing a while, have him do it from farther out, with only one dribble.

The best angle to take is 45 degrees to the hoop. Obviously, there is often no choice. If there is, the player should come in at this angle, since it maximizes ball control and use of the backboard.

5. Get the Proper Footwork. As a player is laying the ball up, she pumps up the knee on the same side as the shooting hand and drives straight up with the opposite foot. Kids often push off the wrong foot, and it's important for them to get the proper footwork right away. If the lay-up is right-handed, then the right arm needs to stretch up, and the whole right side should lift with it. Raising the right knee high does this. The concept is to raise the whole right side on right-handed shots (vice versa for lefty lay-ups). This skill comes after a few practice sessions. Note that this means that, coming off the dribble, the first free step for a right-handed lay-up is with the right foot, and the drive up comes off the left foot.

At the beginning of that step, the player grabs the ball with both hands and prepares to shoot, finally driving off the left foot. Lifting the right knee also adds to the height of the jump. Finally, the player needs to remember to jump straight up. This not only adds to the height of the jump, but it also slows down the forward movement of the body so the ball hits the backboard a bit more softly.

6. Soft Off the Backboard. A player should pick a spot on the backboard and lay the ball up softly off the glass. Because the overwhelming majority of lay-ups are shot off the backboard, you should teach even your youngest players to use it for this shot. The hardest thing about shooting lay-ups is controlling the speed of the ball bouncing off the backboard. Most missed shots arise because the ball hits the backboard too hard as a result of the body's forward speed and momentum. At the youngest ages, nearly all misses are hard shots. Jumping straight up slows the ball a bit, but it still needs to be laid-up softly.

The ball sits in the right hand, the shooter's palm turned partially inward toward him. The shot can be done with the palm outward, like a jump shot, but it's much tougher to con-

3-6. SHOOTING LAY-UPS

When shooting a lay-up, lift the entire right side—leg and arm—and jumps straight up, driving off the left foot. Rotate the body for easier landing.

trol the ball speed. The hand must soften the ball's impact upon the backboard to adjust for the forward motion of the body. This is done by flipping the ball backward a bit to decrease its speed. As a player becomes experienced, he may apply spin to compensate for odd angles.

The backboards are usually marked with a square, just over the hoop, and the player lays the ball up against the lines of that square. Usually, the target is the upper corner of these lines, or just below that point, but it will vary with the player, given her height and softness of shot. Teach the team to find the right spot and hit it every time. With practice, a player will shoot automatically and not need to focus on the square.

Next, the body rotates or twists counterclockwise a bit to prepare for a controlled landing. This rotation should be coached, but don't confuse things too much in the early stages. Just tell your child to twist a bit in order to land on-balance.

Other Options

1. Dish the Ball Off if Needed. We mentioned that once the ball handler successfully passes a defender, a big player underneath will react to defend his teammate. If this happens, the defender has abandoned and opened up the man he was guarding. Your player continues with the lay-up, inciting the big defender to commit fully, and then she dishes (passes) the ball off to the open player. It works like a charm!

2. Practice the Lefty Shot. Be patient here since, for righties, developing a lefty lay-up is the toughest thing in basketball. Start slowly. Urge your players to try it a few times. It will feel very awkward, and progress will be slow. To execute a lefty shot, reverse the footwork. On the left side of the basket, a lefty shot is more effective since it places the body between the defender and the ball. That's why all your players should be comfortable doing it.

3. Be Fancy. Some coaches discourage kids from shooting trick or fancy, off-balance lay-ups during practice, but I never does. In a game, the defender usually doesn't allow a textbook shot, so the shooter often needs to contort a bit. Therefore, this situation should be practiced. Let the kids have fun with it once in a while. Use the hang time, the air time, to double pump, twist, and change angles.

SHORT JUMP SHOTS

Short jump shots, called chippies when I played, get blocked most often because they are shot in close to the hoop where the big players roam, and the shooter doesn't have the advantage of body motion that a lay-up provides.

The mechanics of short shots are similar to those of longer outside shots, except that the player needs to be much more concerned about the defender. The shot needs to be carried out very quickly, with quick moves and quick release.

Fakes are even more important in close to the hoop. The best fake is for the shooter to raise the ball quickly as if to shoot, get the defender to jump, and then go up as she comes down. Sometimes, a few fake pumps with the ball are needed to get the defender to react. Often the shooter can catch the defender coming forward off-balance and lean into her to draw a foul.

Often a short jump shot can effectively use the backboard. It's a bit tougher, but it provides a lighter, off-line arc, which is harder to defend. Ordinarily, any shot within four to five feet of the hoop and to the side should use the backboard. Jumpers in front of the hoop go directly to the rim. Remind your player to focus on the point of the rim closest to her and to arc the ball softly to that spot. A dish off to an open player can also be a very effective alternative to shooting in traffic.

THE HOOK SHOT

The hook shot is pretty much a big player's shot because it is used underneath the hoop. Usually, the shot occurs when an outside player passes to the shooter, whose back is initially to the hoop. The shooter turns sideways to the hoop, fakes a turn one way, usually with the head and shoulders, then leans the other way, pivoting on one

03

3-7. **HOOK SHOT**

Underneath the hoop, the hook is an essential shot.

foot (off the right foot for a righty hook and the left foot for a lefty hook), and jumping with strength from the opposite foot (or hopping and jumping off both feet). The legs should feel balanced. If the defender is moving, the shooter leans into him.

In preparation to shoot, the player should bring the ball up the right side of the body, hold it tightly, then raise it with the right hand away from the defender, protecting it with the other forearm and the other side of the body. The shooter should focus on the closest point of the hoop, look at it specifically, then flick the ball over it softly. Hook shots from the middle usually do not use the backboard. If the hook comes in from one side of the hoop, a bank shot is better.

They key here is to jump aggressively and look at the nearest point on the rim. A big player must develop a hook shot. It's tough to defend and can be very accurate if practiced. Like all shots, it should be practiced.

FOUL SHOTS (OR FREE THROWS)

Foul shots (or free throws) certainly deserve special mention. It can be said that foul shooting wins or loses most close games, and this is so at all levels of play. At beginner ages, good foul shooting is rare, and, in clinics, fouls are often not called. But when the kids start shooting free throws, since scores are usually low, a good foul shooter can win a game.

A player get two free shots if he is fouled in the act of shooting and the shot is missed and one foul shot if the shot is made. Two shots are also awarded for any

46

intentional or flagrant foul. One shot and possession of the ball is awarded for technical fouls, such as excessive shouting by the coach, foul language, or unsportsmanlike conduct. If fouled in any other manner, a player gets to shoot only if the other team has accumulated seven personal fouls during the half. In these cases, one foul shot is awarded, and a second bonus shot is awarded if the first shot scores. This is called a one-and-one. Upon the opponent's tenth team foul, two free throws are awarded.

In lining up for foul shots, two defenders take the positions closest to the hoop, between the block and the first lane markers, on both sides of the lane. Two of the shooter's teammates line up next, followed by two defenders. (See figure 3-8.) The remaining defender and an opponent usually line up near mid-court to prepare for a defensive rebound and subsequent play toward the other end of the court. The fifth offensive player usually hovers in the wing area. The shooter stands on the free-throw line, which some programs may shorten from the regulation fifteen-foot distance for younger kids.

Players may enter the foul lane after the ball leaves the shooter's hand, but the shooter can't enter the lane until the ball touches the rim or backboard.

Shooting foul shots is much like shooting jump shots, except the feet don't leave the ground. In the old days, players like the great Wilt Chamberlain used to shoot fouls underhanded with two hands. However, the highest percentage shots, as said before, are one-handed flicks from a cradle. The ball is brought over the head, cradled, and shot

3–8. FREE THROW LINE-UP

Shooter's opponents get the spots closest to the hoop. His teammates get the next spots. Opponents get the third position.

with one hand. The shooting hand ends up in a gooseneck, just as with jump shots. The head and shoulders are square to the hoop. The shooting elbow points at the hoop.

Much of foul shooting comes from the legs. They must bend and extend into the shot. The body starts low and fully extends, up on the toes, and the player stays up on the toes while the ball is in flight. The key is for the shooter to stay extended into the shot. The entire motion is fluid and continuous, and the player follows through, giving the ball a nice reverse 30-degree rotation.

It's also important to point the front foot, usually the right foot for a righty shot, at the hoop. The shooter should line up the foot in the middle of the foul stripe, pointed at the center of the hoop. There is usually a nail hole or marking in the middle of the stripe which provides a good point of reference, although some players obtain greater accuracy left or right of it. The key is to do position the foot the exact same way each time. Think that the foot, elbow, and forefinger are all aligned with the centerpoint on the hoop.

The other foot can be back a slight, but comfortable, distance, at a 45-degree angle. Remember, as with all shooting, the player shoots with the legs. He should also make sure his hands are dry and shake any tenseness out of the wrists and fingers. He should grip the ball so it's comfortable.

Foul shots should be practiced, preferably a minimum of twenty-five, at the end of each practice session, while the player is tired. Shooting while tired simulates game conditions. A nice high arc is best, so players should find one that's comfortable.

The final concept in foul shooting is to relax, take a deep breath, and dribble a few times. I tell players to line up the ball in their hands the same way each time and dribble it to the same spot on the floor to get that "automatic" feeling. They then picture the shot going in and shoot with a positive attitude. The shooter's last thought should be, "It's going in."

SHOOTING DRILLS

PARENTS FEEDING PASSES

The best way to practice shooting is just to do it! The great shooters practiced for hours a day as kids. Players need to get the mechanics working properly and then shoot thousands of shots. Kids won't get to practice shooting much at team practices, as I said, so they have to do it on their own. This is where the parent can be most helpful. A parent can rebound and feed the pass back to his child for another shot, doing many repetitions in a relatively short time. I did this for a summer once with my older son, and his shot accuracy improved dramatically. Feeding passes for shots

3-9. FEEDING REBOUNDS

Probably the most helpful and easiest practice a parent can provide is to feed her child rebounds.

is the absolute best practice drill there is. Believe me, I did it ten thousand times … easy! It may be the best help you can give to a child at any level, since it allows for many shots in a very short period of time. The parent should remind the child to point her shooting foot, hand, and elbow; cradle; flick the wrist; use soft, relaxed hands; keep her eyes on the front of the rim (the point of the rim closest to the child); keep the head and shoulders fairly square; shoot quickly; release quickly; jump higher; fake the dribble, follow up the shot; shoot with confidence; shoot from the legs; feel graceful. After a while, the parent will chase far fewer rebounds! (See figure 3-9.)

After a while, the parent should play a little defense on the child as he shoots and then go back for the rebound. The child can fake and drive, while the parent applies enough pressure to make it challenging, but not overwhelming.

Ultimately, a game of one-on-one is great practice. I used to defend against my son at nine years old, and I would not use my hands to defend his shots (my head was about as high as a kid's hand and supplied sufficient pressure). I also would not raise my hands above my head to rebound—it kept things more even.

EARLIER DRILLS

I won't repeat them here, but don't forget to include the specialty shooting drills listed in chapter two, such as Rapid Shooting, Medley Shooting, Corner Shots, and Wing

Shots. Also, the Wall Drill and the Fake-Away Drill discussed earlier in this chapter are great teaching drills.

DRILLS FOR PRACTICE

There are several form drills that can be employed early in the season. Coaches should practice the triple-threat stance in conjunction with these drills.

21-Jumper Drill. This drill practices shooting and following up shots. Two teams of two players each are positioned for fifteen-foot jump shots. A player on each team shoots, follows up for the rebound, and passes back to his teammate who in turn shoots and rebounds. This continues until a team gets 21 points (one for each shot).

21-Lay-Up Drill. This drill is like 21 Jumper, except the players drive from beyond the foul line and do lay-ups. After rebounding, the player passes to her teammate and runs to the opposite side of the basket from which she just shot to await her turn. This ensures she will alternate righty and lefty lay-ups. Lay-ups done from the left side must be shot lefty. You might stand under the hoop to ensure that players jump straight up. You can also apply some pressure to simulate game conditions under the hoop and to encourage a firm ball grip.

Run-and-Jump Drill. This drill practices jump shots from a dribble. Guards line up in the middle of the half-court line, and forwards line up along the sideline twenty feet from the end line. Guards dribble to any point fifteen feet from the hoop, stop quickly, and jump shoot. Forwards dribble toward the corner and do the same. This drill can also be done along a fifteen-foot semicircle, but make sure players dribble a few times before shooting. Each must follow the shot and get his own rebound. After a while, you can place defenders along the inside of this perimeter to apply light defense.

50-Freebies Drill. Players should try to make fifty foul shots a day; one hundred is better. Two players take turns shooting ten shots at a time until they've made fifty shots. For younger athletes, adjust the number. The other player rebounds and then shoots when it's her turn.

Tapping Drill. Pick a spot on a wall about 11 feet off the ground and have the players keep tapping to it. Vary the distance and have the players move left and right to get different angles. Players should hit the spot at the top of the arc. A variation is to position two players under either side of the hoop. One throws the ball off the backboard or rim for the other to tap in. Then the second player throws it up for the first player to tap in. Have them switch sides.

50

DRIBBLING

04

The most important team skill in youth basketball is dribbling, so it follows that the most important thing you can do as a coach is to teach and emphasize this. How often do we see a youngster out on a basketball playground, standing there shooting, just shooting, and nothing else? And then, how often do we see players in a game that can't dribble an inch, becoming easy prey for quick defensive hands.

Sure, shooting is very important. It is the purpose of the game. But good passing is even more important to team success, and dribbling is most important. Few people seem to understand this, and it is most unfortunate when coaches don't. Players simply can't shoot if they can't get the ball close to the hoop.

Dribbling is a purely individual skill, and it is the most important initial step in the development of a young basketball player. It is definitely the best confidence builder. A boy or girl who can move with the basketball will be valuable to the team and will also be able to develop other skills more quickly. As stated earlier, at beginner levels, teaching kids to dribble is clearly the biggest challenge a coach faces.

4-1. DRIBBLING: THE BEST YOUTH SKILL

A young player who can dribble will quickly become the team leader. It is a most important skill in youth basketball.

THE IMPORTANCE OF DRIBBLING FOR BEGINNERS

Children typically begin playing basketball in clinic-type programs for a few years prior to fifth or sixth grade, when school or tournament teams are formed. Observe these programs, and you'll quickly notice that confusion reigns on the court. Few shots are taken because the ball is constantly being stolen. A child will get the ball and just freeze. He will be immediately surrounded by opposing players and will either throw the ball away or have it swiped from his hands. Scores are often in the single figures.

The standout on the floor is the child who does not freeze but who can dribble the ball around the other players. This child can then advance for a good shot or pass the ball to an open teammate. Thus, confidence grows, all skills become developed, and a basketball player emerges. Dribbling is the ticket! When children lack this skill, they are somewhat afraid of the ball. You can see they don't want the ball, and they lack confidence when they have it. Have your players practice dribbling to address this problem, and the result will be a bounty of self-assurance.

So get your player to work on dribbling and handling the ball, both during team practice and at home. When my youngest son was eight years old, I cleared out a small area in the basement (it's cold outside during basketball season in New Jersey), a space of about 10' x 10', but even a smaller space would have been okay. He would go down for twenty minutes and practice dribbling. I told him to make sudden moves, perform

4-2. PRACTICE DRIBBLING

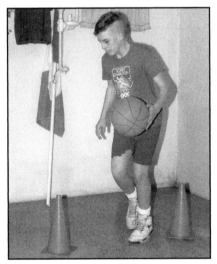

Practicing in the cellar is a ticket to great progress.

52

figure-eights, dribble behind his back, set up obstacles and dribble around them, and practice dribbling with both his right and left hands. After a while, I would put some pressure on him, trying to steal the ball. We set up a runway between cellar rooms so he would get some speed for a twenty-foot speed dribble. In a very short time, he improved significantly, and the improvement was quite noticeable as he played in the clinic. Don't expect miracles; expect improvement! It will come.

On warmer days, we would go outside. Any hard, flat surface is okay: side streets (watch the cars), sidewalks, a driveway. It's not necessary to have a basket to practice dribbling. Have your son or daughter start by dribbling back and forth over a fifty-foot distance, right-handed one way, left-handed coming back. Tell parents of your players to urge this kind of practice to their children.

THE TOP TEN FUNDAMENTALS OF DRIBBLING

1. Finger Control. The ball is dribbled with the fingers, particularly the thumb and the three middle fingers. Some kids initially use the palm of the hand. However, the palm has only a limited role in helping the fingers to receive and cradle the ball. The fingers do most of the work. The ball should be out on the fingers and the upper palm near the fingers as much as possible. The upper palm and lower thumb area often receive the bounced ball, especially if the player is on the run, but then the fingertips take over. They direct the downward dribble as the ball rolls off the fingertips.

4-3. **DRIBBLE WITH THE FINGERS**

Dribbling is done with the fingers and the upper palm.

53

2. Receive, Cradle, and Pump. When little kids start dribbling for the first time, their natural impulse is to strike the ball downward when dribbling, bouncing it. Their hand should not strike the ball; rather, the hand softens and receives the ball well before the top of its bounce, cradles it for a split second, maximizing the time of contact with the hand or *feel*, then pumps it back to the floor. The hand actually withdraws as it meets the ball, so it catches the ball, controls it, and then directs it down again. Often in dribbling, the player needs to make sudden moves or change speeds. The hand needs to have sufficient contact and control so that these moves can be made. This kind of control helps the player send the ball back out in the desired direction, with appropriate velocity. (See figure 4-4.)

The point of contact between the hand and the ball varies, depending on the direction the player takes. Usually, the index and middle fingers are on top of the ball, with the fingertips at or just forward of the uppermost point of the ball's curve. However, if the player is running with the ball, the fingers make contact farther back from the top center so they can push the ball forward. If a left turn is needed, then the fingers cradle the ball more from the right side. In the past, rules against cradling the ball from underneath, also called carrying or palming, were stricter. Fouls for palming, in which the palm and fingers completely "carry" the ball for a while, seem to be called less frequently these days, unless the violation is flagrant, but coaches should still emphasize dribbling without palming.

3. Move With Rhythm. In order for a player to dribble well, her entire arm and shoulder should move in a pumping action, rising at the shoulder and bending at the elbow. The concept you want to teach is one of rhythm. The arm pumps in rhythm with the ball's bouncing. This rhythm is the essence of dribbling.

First, get your players to understand the rhythm between the pumping action of the arm and the ball's bouncing. Get them to think about that rhythm while practicing. During a game, they won't have time to think about it, but if they practice regularly, it will become natural.

The next step is for the player to get her entire body moving in the same rhythm; that is, hook her feet into the pumping of the arm and the bouncing of the ball. The concept is the same. The entire body must move in the same rhythm.

Stutter-Step Drill. A good drill for developing rhythm is the stutter step. Have your players spread their legs, left foot forward, and move forward half or full court with a small hopping or stutter step, in rhythm with the ball. Tell them to "feel" the rhythm.

4-4. **RECEIVE, CRADLE, AND PUMP**

Step 1: The steps to good dribbling are receive, cradle, and pump. The player's fingers extend to receive the ball.

Step 2: Receive. The fingertips receive the ball and begin to withdraw.

Step 3: Cradle. The arm and hand withdraw a bit, cradling the ball at the top of the bounce.

Step 4: Pump. The hand pumps the ball back down.

55

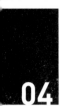

The left foot is always forward when dribbling righty, since that also is the best posture to shield the ball, but small steps are taken, pushing off the back foot. This drill builds the sense of rhythm so essential to good dribbling. If your child practices in the basement, turn on a radio and have her dribble-dance to the beat of the music.

4. Develop Both Hands. If a player can dribble with only one hand, his ability to move will always be limited. Defenders usually lean to their left a bit to cut off the space to the dribbler's right. The ability to then switch to the left hand and drive to the left side opens a whole new dimension and substantially improves a player's offensive potential. You need to continually remind your players to use both hands. Don't nag, just encourage them to devote some time to the other hand. Use drills to get them started.

If a player is a righty, have him spend time using only the left hand. When you apply pressure to his right side, be sure he attempts the left-handed drive. It will be difficult, sloppy, and awkward for him at first, so be supportive. Remind him that he will improve; praise the first sign of improvement. Remind him how hard it seemed to learn to whistle or ride a bike at first, and how easy it was once he got the hang of it.

5. Head Up, Eyes Looking Forward. A child initially dribbles with her head down, keeping the ball in her field of vision. As she improves and develops a feel for the ball and its rhythm, she will be able to direct her attention more to what's going on around her. To the extent she keeps her head down, she will be unaware of opportunities around her: who is open for a pass, what lane is available for advancing the ball, which way the defender is leaning, what opportunities are developing from the flow of play.

I wouldn't harp on this too much. The player's head will come up as he becomes experienced enough to know where the ball is, by feel instead of by sight. You need to talk about the concept and why it's helpful to be able to focus on the whole floor. Read the section on floor vision in chapter two. There are practice techniques that can help, such as having your players close their eyes while dribbling, in order to force them into more reliance on feeling the ball's motion. Patience is needed here, since much practice is required before their feel of the ball is sufficiently developed. It is useful, however, to remind your players, every once in a while, to try to lift their attention, to be more broadly aware of what's going on around them. Guards need to practice this skill regularly.

6. Keep Everything Low. Players should keep the ball low in traffic, the body balanced and relaxed. A high, bouncing dribble is easy to steal in traffic. Also, the longer the ball is away from the player's hand, the fewer opportunities she will have to change direction or react quickly. During practice, and especially during drills, remind your players to keep the ball, the dribbling hand, the dribbling elbow, and the body's center of gravity low.

Players should practice keeping the dribble at knee height. Have them observe and feel the differences between a high and low dribble. In a low dribble, the tempo and rhythm are much faster and the ball is more under control. (See figure 4-5.)

The body should always feel balanced and graceful, with weight forward on the balls of the feet. Staying in touch with the rhythm of the ball and staying relaxed help greatly. The great players make basketball look effortless because they are balanced, relaxed, in touch with the ball, and confident in their ability.

For speed dribbling, the ball bounces much higher. The hand pushes the ball out in front, just a bit to the side. High dribbles are for speed; low dribbles are to maintain possession.

7. Shield the Ball. A player needs to keep her body between the ball and the defender. This is called shielding. If the dribbler keeps her body between the defender and the ball, the defender can't get to the ball without fouling. Again, shielding is more easily done if the player can dribble well with both hands. While the dribbling elbow is in close, the other elbow is out shielding the body (but ensure she doesn't push with it). (See figure 4-6.) Shielding is an essential skill and should be practiced at beginner levels.

4-5. DRIBBLE LOW

Low dribbles are hard to steal and much easier to control.

4-6. SHIELD THE BALL WITH THE BODY

A player should use her shoulder and hip to shield the ball, but be careful not to foul the defender.

Shield Drill. Have a dribbler and a defender line up at the top of the key and dribble to the baseline. The dribbler uses his body to shield the ball, backing up, faking a move one way and going the other, switching hands. The defender should not foul. Have the dribbler try to get to the baseline without losing the ball.

8. Buy Time with Pivots. You will see it happen at beginner levels a million times. A player gets the ball, hesitates too long, and quickly becomes closely guarded. She freezes and loses the ball. An easy move that can buy some time is the pivot, moving the body and ball into open space to get more time to pass to a teammate. Pivots can be used before dribbling or after to buy time if needed.

Sure, often a player will receive a pass on the run, such as a mid-court pass, the final pass in a give-and-go play, or a cutting move to the hoop. In these situations, she should continue to use her momentum and speed to its best advantage. If there is a free lane in front of the player, it's almost always best to move directly through it and advance the ball. Often, however, a player will receive a pass while closely guarded. This requires her to put a move on the defender, get the defender to lean or commit to one side, and then quickly dribble the other way while the defender is off balance. The player fakes to one side and goes to the opposite. However, if advancing the ball is not possible, then a player will become closely guarded and needs to maneuver somehow to make a pass. The best move at this time is a pivot.

For some reason, kids tend to learn the pivot concept slowly, and this severely limits their range of opportunity. They feel that their feet can move only while dribbling. The pivot rule, however, allows a player to pivot freely on one foot. The toes of the pivot foot cannot leave the floor and cannot slide, but they can rotate as much as needed, and the heel may leave the floor. A player closely guarded by a defender can pivot 180 degrees in order to get the defender behind her, thus protecting the ball. (See figure 4-7.) A pivot can be part of a fake, with the player stepping sharply in one direction to get a defender off balance, then pivoting back the other direction. Pivots can be a quarter turn, a 180-degree turn, or a full 360-degree turn. Pivoting, or turning, requires you to keep one foot, your pivot foot, stationary. A player who has pivoted on one foot cannot change and pivot on the other foot without a dribble. Pivot fundamentals include: taying in a low, triple-threat position, swinging the ball and arms in the direction of the pivot to help quickness, spinning on the balls of the pivot foot, and keeping the elbows out once the defender is behind or beside you to protect the ball.

58

4-7. **THE PIVOT**

Step 1: The pivot rule lets the ballhandler rotate 180 degrees on her toes in order to get the defender behind her. As the defender approaches, the ballhandler first establishes the left foot as the pivot.

Step 2: To protect the ball, the ballhandler pivots counterclockwise on the left toes, away from the defender.

04

Pivot Drill. Divide the team up into equal sized pairs, and have players alternate guarding each other closely. (Don't let them foul.) Give each player twenty to thirty seconds to pivot multiple times away from the pressure to get the feel of the full range of pivot opportunities. Remind them that, normally, they must pass in five seconds if closely guarded, but here you want them to get the feel of how helpful pivoting can be. Switch after twenty to thirty seconds and have the other player pivot. After a while, when they are ready, have two players guard the pivoter so she learns what can be done in such a situation to buy time.

9. Fakes Make Space. There are several types of fakes. Keep in mind that most fakes require the player be able to dribble with either hand. Once a defender knows your player can dribble only to one side, then any fakes to the other side are not effective.

Full-Body Fake. The most common fake is a full-body fake. Here, using the right foot as a pivot, the player steps sharply toward the left, bringing the body and ball to the left. He then pivots quickly back to the right, crossing the left foot over to the right and then exploding into the open space driving off the pivot foot. This works in the opposite direction as well. The idea behind any fake is for the player to make the defender believe he will move one way, so she follows him. I find it useful to teach the

4–8. **THE FULL-BODY FAKE**

Step 1: The full-body fake requires a sharp step to the left with the entire body. Get the defender to lean that way.

Step 2: The ballhandler then drives to the opposite side, pushing off with the left foot and crossing it over to the right, around the defender.

they are actually pulling the defender off balance, and then suddenly change direction. The direction change must be very quick in order to dart through the lane opened by the fake. Tell your players to drive right by and as close to the defender as possible. They should aggressively step into and claim the lane, leaving only inches between them and the defender. If the defender comes back too hard, she will commit a foul.

Sometimes it helps to make a short jab step to see what the defender will do, then follow it with an explosive step past the defender in the same direction. The jab step sets the defender up into thinking the player will not go that way, and that's the best time to do just that.

Head, Shoulder, or Ball Fake. The head, shoulder, or ball fake is a variation of the fuller fake. The idea is to fake the head, the shoulder, the ball, or any combination of these three, just to get the defender to hesitate, and then very quickly snap back the other way.

Double Fake. The double fake includes a half-hearted fake one way and a full, intensive fake the other, with the player using quick pivot action. If the defender thinks he has picked up the first fake and goes the other way, your player should head in the direction of the first fake. The idea is not so much to plan a series of fakes but rather to feel the defender's balance and take advantage of the first mistake he makes. Footwork for this needs to be practiced a lot so it is smooth.

Shot or Pass Fake. The shot, or pass, fake is probably the most effective fake in basketball. The player pretends to take a jump shot, actually cradling the ball and seeming to begin to shoot (without the pivot foot leaving the ground) and then, as the defender comes forward or jumps to defend the shot, she simply dribbles around him. Young players fall for this often! It's important for the player to look at the basket and really pretend to shoot, to get the defender to come forward. Sometimes, the player may only need to raise the ball quickly to get a defender to react. Similarly, a player may pretend to pass the ball to a teammate, hoping the defender will lean toward the pass, and then dribble the opposite way.

Feint. Another effective fake is a feint, or change in speed, while dribbling. The player pretends to speed up with a big, explosive step and then slows down suddenly. This is also called a hesitation move: Dribble fast, then hesitate, then explode. Often the defender will be caught off balance. Any change in speed while dribbling can be quite effective in unbalancing a defender.

Fake-and-Shake Drills. Have the players line up, in two lines if you have another coach, and go through a few body fakes each. Then have them practice some ball or

shooting fakes. The coach applies very light pressure, going with the fake. Work primarily on footwork, pivoting, cross-overs, and exploding through the lane. Have them start in slow motion to get the footwork down, then slowly increase quickness.

10. Don't Pick Up the Dribble. Perhaps the most common mistake youngsters make, once they get the ball, is to stop dribbling without an available shooting or passing opportunity. The result is usually that defenders quickly swoop in to try and grab the ball.

Often this occurs as a player gets into a bit of traffic and then reacts by stopping to see who he can pass to. This problem arises out of inexperience and because the player's dribbling skills aren't quite good enough for them to simultaneously dribble and look up to see who is open. So, the first step is to make sure the player is dribbling with his head up, not looking at the ball. If he runs into traffic and no pass is open, he should shield the ball with his body between it and the defender and then dribble to open space. The keep-away drill below is helpful in teaching a player to keep dribbling while under pressure.

Keep-Away Drill. Two players stay inside a ten-foot square. One dribbles. One tries to get the ball. This drill teaches how to use the body to shield the ball.

OTHER DRIBBLING DRILLS

I've touched on a couple of drills already in this chapter. I also introduced some in chapter two, such as the sprint dribble for guards. The best way to learn to dribble is just to practice and keep practicing it. Much can be done at home, since dribbling practice needs only a hard surface. In cold weather, players can practice in the basement or garage on a concrete floor; in warmer weather, they can dribble on the driveway or sidewalk. Practice can include just fooling around with the ball, switching hands, sudden movements (behind the back, between the legs), and speed dribbling; the players should use both hands, use two balls, close the eyes, practice fakes.

Many of these drills should be demonstrated once; then you can urge the kids to do them all on their own. Teach them what to do and tell them that personal practice will perfect the skill. Parents can help during at-home practice sessions by creating pressure situations. The parent stands as an obstacle for their child to dribble around or attempts to steal the ball. They should apply enough pressure to make it a challenge but not dominate. Win a few, lose a few. Make it fun!

Cone Drill. Set up a half-dozen or more cones in a line about four to six feet apart and have players dribble, weaving through the cones. When a player gets to the end, she

4-9. **CONE DRILL**

Cone dribbling is a great drill that requires players to dribble while weaving through the cones. Players can be timed, and they can also practice with both hands.

speed dribbles back. They start over again. Use a stopwatch or a watch with a second hand to measure the best time and then have them run against the clock. Have players do a series, switching the ball from right- to left-handed dribbling.

Zigzag Drill. Similar to the cone drill, the players zigzag back and forth while they dribble upcourt. Cones are not necessary, but they can help young players. Each zig should be about eight to twelve feet, depending on age.

One-On-One Drill. Let your players start at the top of the key, dribbling against you or another coach. Have each player put a fake on you as you defend, and then drive toward the basket for a lay-up. Apply light pressure.

King-of-the-Hill Drill. Several players dribble in a square area (or the circle around the foul line) and try to tap each other's ball away with one hand, while dribbling with the other. The last one "alive" wins.

Dribble-Race Drill. Divide players into two or three teams, and have them form lines at one end of the court. The lead player in each line must dribble-race to the other end and return, handling the ball to the next in line, who then repeats the sprint-dribble. Have the players do the second race left-handed.

Double-Up Drill. Have players dribble with two balls at the same time, in the same rhythm, trying to lengthen the time they can do so without losing a ball. This is a great drill.

63

Lay-Down Drill. Players dribble while lying on their side, sitting on the floor, or kneeling. All these drills are designed to give them different feels. Have the players take ten seconds for each position, each hand.

Foolin'-Around Drill. Players dribble behind the back, or between the legs, while walking. Another drill is for the players to stand still and pass the ball back and forth quickly off the fingers. You can also have the players, while dribbling, bounce the ball harder and harder, trying to control it. Again, the idea is to give different feels for the ball, getting the player comfortable with all variations and touches. Have them try dribbling with their eyes closed for a while and with alternate hands. They can try spinning the ball on a finger.

4-10. **HAVE FUN**

Do different things to keep players interested.

PASSING

Nothing is more helpful to team play than good, snappy passing. A child will play less if he tends to throw the ball away, so he must learn the importance of accurate and quick pass work. A bad pass causes the receiver to lose momentum and usually results in a lost shooting opportunity or a turnover, that is, losing the ball to the opponent.

A good pass can set up an easy shot. As stated in the second chapter, kids often just want to go out and shoot, shoot, shoot. I have no problems with shooting, as long as it is put in perspective and other skills are also developed. Good dribbling and good passing lead to good shots. The great ball players—Bob Cousy, Magic Johnson, Larry Bird—were better known for their incredible passing than for anything else. As I look back at my own playing days under the hoop, the times I scored a lot occurred when my team had a really good passing guard. His passes gave me easy shots underneath, so he made me look good.

PASSING IN YOUTH BALL

Unfortunately, passing is the nemesis of youth basketball. It is a team skill, so it requires "two to tango." If either the passer or the receiver makes a mistake, the ball can easily be lost to the opposing team. At the very young ages, passing is quite bad, and confusion reigns. In most clinic programs for the very young beginners, players are not allowed to press; that is, they must allow the opposing team to move the ball past the mid-court line before they can defend or try to steal. Were it not for such a rule, the kids would rarely get the ball very far upcourt.

Actually, the biggest problems with passing in youth basketball are inexperience and the lack of confidence that inexperience brings. A kid gets the ball and freezes. He feels awkward and clumsy. Opposing players take advantage of the hesitation and close in on him. He does not know how to dribble out of the situation. He panics a bit,

closes off his awareness of his teammates, and doesn't see them for a pass. Often, the player will just pivot, turn his back to the defender, and cover up the ball. As a result, the ball is stolen from his hands or an opponent gets a hand on the ball, and a jump ball is called. If the player is closely guarded and holds the ball for more than five seconds, he loses the ball on a five-second violation. Another result may be that he just makes a bad pass. Chances are, you will see some of your players in this situation. If you do, relax; it is common. It occurs because your kids have not played enough. Make sure you tell them this and suggest they resolve to work a bit harder to improve basic skills.

THE LONG, LONG ROAD

There is no quick cure to this problem. Dribbling practice will allow the player to dribble out of jams, keep her head up, and open her focus or attention to the whole floor, as stated in chapter four. Once a player has stopped dribbling, the pivot moves will effectively protect the ball and buy her time to spot an open teammate for a pass. The pivot should not be just a cover-up, however, as it is preferable to face the defender strongly, fake him, and dribble or pass around him. You can teach the kids plays based on prearranged patterns of movement, the main idea of which is to get a player open for a pass and an easy shot. It helps a player to know ahead of time where teammates are supposed to be, so he can anticipate where his pass should go. Eventually, as as time goes on, players begin to know each other's moves.

You need to be patient here. Good passing can only be developed with experience. It's important to teach your players to look for the open teammate. Ball-hogs don't last long in basketball. No matter how good they are, they are not good for the team if they won't pass. Teammates eventually retaliate and won't give the ball to a ball-hog. It always leads to trouble. If a player gets this way, you must try to help change his approach. It's not enough that he is better than the other kids, if that is indeed true. You must help him understand that only team players survive in the long run.

On the other hand, there are some kids who always pass. They don't try to dribble; they never try to shoot. They just don't want the ball! If a child falls into this pattern, don't be alarmed. Many kids do. However, you need to build up her confidence. Words are helpful, but they are empty unless she regularly practices ball-handling skills.

There is no quick fix for any passing problem. However, regular practice will definitely result in improvement. You need to believe this if your players are to believe it. I live right next to an outdoor basketball court, and over the years I have seen various children from the neighborhood on the court. The ones who show up most often improve and become decent ball players. Pretty soon, they are varsity high-school players.

It's as simple as that. Practice and repetition work. One need not be "born with it." It's like learning how to type. It seems impossible at first, but with practice and experience, it becomes second nature. It can be learned. So can basketball skills!

So when it comes to passing, setting up a good pass is the key. Good passing is less a technical skill and more the result of good individual or team dynamics. There are, however, some basic fundamentals for passing and receiving the ball.

THE TOP TEN FUNDAMENTALS OF PASSING

The two-handed chest pass is by far the predominant pass in basketball, so I will use it to describe the fundamentals of passing.

1. Use Two Hands. A basketball is pretty big; it's tough to control with only one hand. The activity on the court is fast and furious and full of sudden movements. Nearly all short- or mid-range passes are two-handed, and the main reason for this is so that a player can control the ball as it is passed. A one-handed pass can roll off the hand as it is thrown. Control the pass with two hands.

A more important reason to use two hands is that passes must happen very quickly. The ball is usually already in front of the player's body, and she had no time to wind up for a one-handed pass. The ball is passed from the front of the torso, and the second hand is needed to give strength and power to the pass.

Obviously, a full-court pass needs the full power of an extended arm and must be thrown like a baseball. Otherwise, use both hands.

2. The Spread-W Hand Position. In this position, the players spread his fingers and rotates his hand up toward the chest area. Holding the ball at its sides, he spreads the thumb and index finger to form an oval with each other, with the thumbs slightly separated, forming a shallow "W" or oval. The other fingers are spread at a relaxed distance from each other, not too far apart. This hand position maximizes both the player's control of the ball and the power coming through the fingers. (See figure 5-1, step 1.)

3. Rotate Up to the Chin. When a ball is caught or taken up from the dribbling position, the player's hands are on the side, fingers out and thumbs up; and the ball is usually waist high. The player begins the passing motion by bringing her hands up and back to the upper chest, just below the chin. The fingers rotate upward and a bit back toward the upper chest as far as is comfortable. When the hands rotate, the elbows spread a bit to get more shoulder strength into the ball. The farther the hands rotate, the more power can be placed

5-1. TWO-HAND CHEST PASS

Step 1: The two-hand chest pass gives your player maximum control of the ball. First, player forms an oval with the thumbs and index fingers.

Step 2: Rotate the ball and fingertips up and into the chest area, to ensure power in the pass.

Step 3: Drive the ball straight out in a whipping action, as the ball rolls off the fingers, and flick the wrists outward.

on the ball as the fingers snap or whip outward. The player drives the ball directly outward in a straight line. Power is transmitted to the pass from the whipping action of the wrists as the ball rolls off the fingers, principally the index finger. The index finger is the center of the pass and is the last finger to touch the ball. (See figure 5-1, steps 2 and 3.)

The player passes the ball from in close to the chest for maximum power. The chest moves forward and down as the player steps toward the target.

68

5-2. STEP INTO THE TARGET

A strong and quick step toward the target adds power and increases control.

4. Step Toward the Target. This action helps both accuracy and power, getting the body in motion with the pass. The step must be very quick, however, so as not to signal the pass and alert the defense to try to steal. The player adds power and accuracy by moving toward the target as much as possible. He should drive the body and hands forward and snap the wrists and fingers outward. This is all one movement done on the balls of the feet.

5. Hit Receivers in the Hands or Chest. The passer wants to get the ball to the receiver's hands. However, it's usually easiest to catch a ball about chest high, and players are supposed to keep their hands up, so in front of the chest is where the hands should be. Obviously, passers shouldn't throw at a teammate's head if his hands are at his waist! If his hands are down, a bounce pass is good. If a receiver is under the hoop, a high pass is more effective, since the player does not need to spend time bringing the ball up. Where the ball needs to be thrown varies, but chest high is the best rule of thumb.

6. Quick and Snappy. The key to successful passing is to get the ball to the receiver before it can be stolen. Passes must be quick and snappy. When drilling your team in passes, you must insist on this. The passer must see the defender and make sure the ball will have enough steam to get by her.

7. Pass to the Open Space: Lead the Receiver. The idea is to pass to the space toward which the receiver is moving. If a player is cutting toward the basket, the passer shouldn't slow him down by passing directly to him; by the time the ball arrives, he will already be a bit past it. So the player must pass to slightly in front of where the receiver is. She

69

should judge the speed of the receiver and pass the ball to meet him, which means she's really passing to open space, anticipating that the receiver will be there.

8. Don't Broadcast the Pass. Good defenders have a knack for anticipating when to intercept passes. The worst thing a player can do on offense, then, is to look right at the target before he makes a pass. He might as well just pass to the defender. The defender knows when his man is open for a pass; he just doesn't know when it's coming. Don't tell him in advance!

After playing a while—it doesn't take long—players develop floor vision. They can see what's going on in front of them without having to focus on any one player. So a passer can see an open teammate without really looking at him. Since he never focuses directly on the receiver, the defensive player is not tipped off. Sometimes, a good passer sees his target and then looks at another player while passing to the first target. This ability is quite valuable, since it gets defenders off balance.

9. Throw Away From the Defender. If a defender is on the right side of the offensive player's target, the pass should be made to the receiver's left so her body shields the ball. Often the receiver will have a hand up to indicate where she wants the ball, and that's the target. If a player is closely guarded, such as in a post-up situation, the pass

5–3. **LEAD THE RECEIVER AWAY FROM THE DEFENDER**

A player should pass the ball to the open space in front of her receiver, so the receiver gets the pass on the run, while moving away from the defender.

70

should be directed to the space away from the defender; ideally, the receiver will have her hand extended into the appropriate space for the pass.

10. React. After a pass, the passer will need to move as directed by the offensive pattern or play being used, but I always tell players to pause a bit, (unless it's a give and go) to make sure the pass gets caught. The passer may be the only line of defense in case of a steal, and he needs to be able to react.

STRESS PASSING TECHNIQUES

Remind your player of these passing techniques as you have a catch or as she passes the ball off a wall. (As a child, I used my cellar wall.) Have her think about her hand position as she catches the ball and then passes it. Have her notice how far back she rotates the hands, and how much more power comes with a greater rotation. Have her notice how much accuracy she gets from stepping toward the target, and the power she gets from driving with the back leg. Tell her to bend forward at the waist for even more power. If she gets the idea of the various building blocks of passing, she will naturally begin to use them. Your job is to make her aware of them and to help her practice them. Even if she is an advanced player, there is no more useful practice than a review of basics and mechanics.

TYPES OF PASSES

The two-handed chest pass I've described is used in the great majority of situations. However, at times, other passes may be needed.

BOUNCE PASS

This pass is good in close situations, when the traffic is heavy. The bounce pass helps to get the ball down under the defender's hands. One problem with the bounce pass is that the floor slows the ball down. Also, this pass needs to be caught fairly low, which is not usually desirable. A player should use this pass only when he needs to get the ball under and past a defender. Topspin helps speed the ball up after it bounces.

OVERHEAD PASS

The two-hand overhead pass is commonly used to get a pass over the head of a defender. It is a very effective pass and is also a good pass fake. The player makes the pass with a quick, inward flick of the wrists and a short step toward the receiver. This pass is

71

used often after a rebound to the outlet player on the wing. The passer holds the ball high over her head, arms fully extended. Her body snaps forward at the waist, and her shoulders snap forward as well. (See figure 5-4.)

BASEBALL PASS

The baseball pass is a one-handed throw, like throwing a baseball. It's used primarily for very long passes, usually as part of a fast break or to break a press. At very young ages, it is not used often, since it's rather hard to catch; for safety reasons, some local rules do not allow it. (See figure 5-5.)

FAKE-SHOT PASS

One of the most effective passes in basketball follows a faked jump shot. Just as the player is poised at the top of his jump, ready to shoot, he passes off to a teammate underneath. The defenders are caught off balance, expecting the shot and beginning to jockey for a possible rebound. The fake-shot pass ensures that the ball gets to the receiver untouched, since defenders don't expect it, and it buys the receiver some time to get the shot off. The

5-4. OVERHEAD PASS

For the overhead pass, player extends the arms overhead and quickly snaps the ball to the receiver.

5-5. THE BASEBALL PASS

The baseball pass is useful for very long passes, such as across or down court.

only problem is that sometimes this fakes out the receiver, and he misses the pass, too! Make sure your players are always alert and ready to receive the ball.

ONE-HANDED PASS

This is like a chest pass, except the player pushes the ball with one hand. It's often used when a player is running, off balance, or whenever the passer can't square up to the receiver. This pass should be the exception, not the rule.

THE TOP FIVE FUNDAMENTALS OF RECEIVING PASSES

The art of passing is mainly in the pass itself. Receiving the pass is not complicated. However, many passes are not caught or are bobbled. These situations are preventable.

1. Know Where the Ball Is and Want It. The most important skill in receiving the pass is simply being alert. Herein lies the greatest difference between the decent ball player and the poor one. A player must always expect and want the ball! Look at any youth basketball game, and you will see that some kids get a lot of loose balls and rebounds and others don't. Some kids seem to never be looking when the ball is passed to them. Some kids never have the ball passed to them because they are not looking, and they don't make eye contact with the passer. These kids don't seem to want the ball. You can see it clearly.

Players should never turn their backs to the ball, unless it's part of a play. They must always know where the ball is and keep it in their field of vision. Most importantly, they should always be prepared to receive a pass, always be looking for the ball—they've got to want it. This is the key!

Kids who want the ball are easy to pick out. They play more aggressively. They are constantly trying to get into position for a pass. Their eyes are on the passer, searching to see if she will pass the ball, signaling they are ready for it with a hand up as a target. They dive for loose balls. Some of this quality seems inborn, but it can be developed. It grows with confidence. Tell your players they must always want the ball. Part of the problem, where there is a problem, comes from lack of confidence. Some kids don't want the ball, because they are afraid they will make a mistake. They somehow manage never to be open for a pass. Deal with this through practice. As skills improve, so does confidence. If a kid plays one-on-one, he will learn what he can do with the ball. He will learn that he can handle the ball, and he will want the ball more often.

73

Scramble Drill. A good drill to make kids go after the ball more aggressively is to line them up on either side of you, a few feet away, and throw the ball softly in various directions—up down, out, roll it, etc.—and have the kids go after it. Match the kids evenly so that no one gets overwhelmed, and tell them to go after the ball (not each other). It's important to start them close to you, so they are not coming directly at each other. This is a great drill for getting kids to go after loose balls.

2. Move to the Ball. The receiver must reach for and, if possible, step to the ball. Defenders will look to steal the pass, so it's important for a receiver to beat them to it. Many, many passes are stolen because the receiver was stationary, waiting for the ball. Teach your players to step to it, at least lean and reach out their hands to receive it! Teach them to claim the ball! (See figure 5-6.)

A good play to set a player up for receiving a pass is the jump stop. The receiver moves to the ball and then, as it is passed, she jumps, receives it in the air, and lands in a triple-threat position, ready to proceed.

Jump-Stop Drill. For beginners, line them up and have them take several quick steps and jump-stop. Then add passing the ball to them, and have them receive it in the air, jumping just as you pass it.

5–6. MOVE TO THE BALL

The most important action in receiving a pass is for the player to move or step to the ball to reach out to receive it. She should see the ball into her hands.

3. Give a Target. It's much easier on the passer if the receiver puts up a hand, palms out, to the spot he wants the ball. For instance, if a defender is on the right side, he should put up a left hand as the target.

4. Soft Hands. A basketball is big and very bouncy, so it's rather difficult to catch. Many kids tense up when the ball approaches, and this increases the chance that the ball will bounce off their hands. Soft hands is a term used in many sports, including baseball, football, and volleyball. (In soccer, the term is soft feet.) Tell your player she must try to relax. Have her shake the hands, loosen them up. Make them less rigid and tense. Have her practice passing and receiving and discuss this concept. Tell her to notice her hands, to make them soft, and then to notice the difference.

5. Keep the Eyes on the Ball. This is the key to catching anything in any sport. The ball is pretty big and easy to see, but that does not lessen the need to concentrate on it. A receiver should watch the ball from the moment it leaves the passer's hands until it's in his hands. He must maintain concentration. It's okay for the player to divide concentration, to begin to sense what to do with the ball, but he should never take his eyes from it. The transition from the catch to the next movement, whether it is a dribble, pass, or shot, requires control of the ball. Control begins with a solid reception. During drills, tell your players to see the ball leave the passer's hands and watch it all the way into their own hands. Tell them to see which way the ball is spinning as it approaches and show you by rotating their fingers. These drills all help to increase concentration.

PASSING DRILLS

I already discussed the best passing drill there is: A parent and a child or two children can just go out and have a catch. You don't need a basket, and you can do this any-where. I used to do it all the time with my sons (just clear away anything breakable!). Passing off a concrete wall is useful for someone who is practicing alone; they should practice hitting various spots.

STRESS THE TECHNIQUES

Talk about the importance of passing as you have a catch. Talk about the techniques, fingers positions, rotation, and stepping to the target. Talk about snappiness and dy-namics. Talk about receiving with soft hands, keeping the eye on the ball, moving to the ball, and keeping body weight forward.

Tip-Tap Drill. A good drill for softening hands is for two players to tip it back and forth between them. I used to stand about five feet from my son, and we would pass the ball quickly back and forth, as quickly as we could, almost tipping it back and forth. This drill forces the child to concentrate on the ball and helps him to develop quicker reflexes.

Monkey-in-the-Middle Drill. This is a good drill because it teaches dribbling, passing, and receiving under pressure. Six players circle the key, a step or so back, with the "monkey" standing in the center of the key. Players can pass to anyone in the circle except the player next to them. They may dribble with the ball, but they can't move more than a few feet to the right or left. The "monkey" tries to intercept a pass or force a turnover. Whoever makes a mistake (five-seconds delay, bad pass, a missed reception, traveling) is the new monkey. Make sure the kids use the pivot move a lot. Watch the fouls; don't let the monkey reach in and foul. To toughen the drill, have each player clap hands once before catching the ball.

Pass Away Drill. This drill is like monkey-in-the-middle, but here it's two-on-two. Set up, using cones or towels, an area 20' x 20'. No dribbling is allowed. The player with the ball may pivot but has only three seconds to pass. The defender counts the seconds out loud by thousands. The receiver must fake and feint to get free. Adjust the area size and timing to fit your players' age group. Younger players need less space.

On the Run Drill. Two players start at one end of the court, or on their sidewalk or driveway, and run to the other end, passing back and forth. No dribbling is allowed, and no traveling is allowed! Only one step is allowed before the ball must be passed. The idea is catch the ball and *immediately* pass it back.

Weaving Drill. Three players run the length of the court in a weaving pattern, as depicted in figure 5-7. The weave is designed so that the ball stays in the center lane of the court. The player with the ball, having received it in the center lane, always passes to another player who is entering the center lane. The passer then runs to the side of the court vacated by the receiver. The receiver then does the same routine, with the player on the other side of the court, and so on.

Players form lines behind #1, #2, and #3. #1 passes to #2, who heads toward the middle lane, ▶ and then #1 (weaves) runs upcourt into the right lane. #2 quickly passes to #3, who has curved toward the center lane, and then #2 weaves behind #3 and continues up the left lane. #3 passes to #1, who has returned to the center lane near mid-court. #1 passes to #2, who comes toward the middle lane from the left lane, and so on, until the last player with the ball shoots a lay-up.

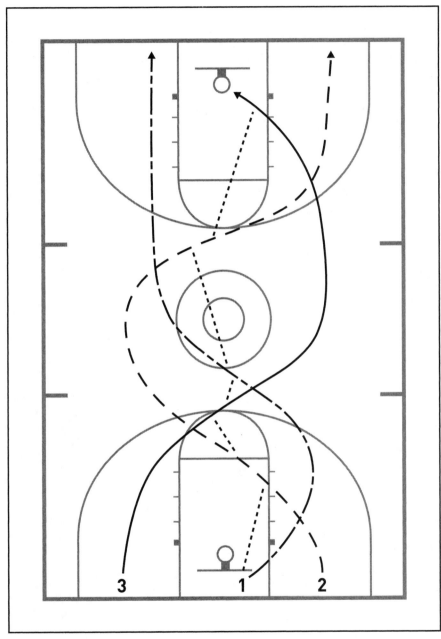

3   1   2

05

Medicine Man Drill. Medicine balls are not used much these days, but they are great passing aides. They are round, stuffed, and leather coated and are both larger and heavier than basketballs. For this drill, position players in two lines, five to ten feet apart, and have them chest-pass and two-hand-overhead pass medicine balls back and forth to build passing strength.

Two-Quick Drill. Two players stand ten to twelve feet apart, each holding a ball. They pass rapidly to each other, one with a chest pass, one with a bounce pass. After a while, they switch pass types.

Finger-Tip Drill. For this simple reflex drill, have players hold the ball between their hands and slowly pass it from hand to hand. They should gradually increase speed to the maximum, still tipping the ball back and forth. See how wide apart they can get their hands at higher speeds.

No-Dribble-Scrimmage Drill. Just what it says: regular scrimmage, no dribbling allowed. This drill forces players to rely on passing.

OFFENSE

06

The first step toward running offensive plays is to understand the reasons for the play. As a coach or a parent, you must develop your players' feel for the game by discussing offensive concepts. Once players understand what a pick is, or a give and go, and why they should use these moves, they will begin to do these things on their own. Once players understand the fundamental moves, you can begin to put these moves together into offensive play patterns, simple at first, and then more complex. Although different coaches will employ different plays, the basic offensive concepts are the same everywhere. In this chapter, I will discuss these concepts and review some specific offensive plays. You and your players should review them together. Initially, most kids don't know anything but how to dribble, pass, and shoot, and an early understanding of concepts will go a long way in getting a kid some extra playing time and that oh-so-necessary experience. We often hear a lot about court sense, and much of it may be innate, but a deep understanding of basic concepts will certainly improve how smartly a kid plays the game.

By far, the most important offensive move is the pick or screen. If you teach nothing else, teach this concept. Talk about why it is important and why and how it helps the team. The concept of the pick is that players can free up a teammate to shoot by screening away his defender. The play is the specific plan designed to set up that screen, (i.e. which player does what). It's all fully choreographed, like a dance. There are different ways to do it, and you could use any of several different players for the screen, but the concept is always the same. Kids need to understand concepts, so they can better react to what's needed in a given situation. Also, understanding concepts helps them understand what you, as their coach, are trying to do with play patterns.

Basketball is somewhere between football and soccer in terms of playmaking. Football has very specific plays that all players follow, with little room for variation, while soccer has far fewer plays and flows from a set of concepts and the opportunities of the moment. Basketball more equally blends both plays and concepts by starting off with a definite play pattern but often resulting in an opportunity for players to make something happen on their own.

THE TOP TEN OFFENSIVE CONCEPTS

Offense grows out of defense, so scoring starts with a defensive rebound or a steal. It includes being able to control the ball through good passing while bringing it up the floor.

The objective of the offense is for your players to move around the court in such a way that one of them is finally in position to take a high-percentage shot. If you have a dominant, big player, your emphasis should be to have the team get her open and pass the ball to her under the basket. If you have a great outside shooter, then run plays that will free her from her defender for a shot. If you have a great dribbler, build plays around that ability, using screens that free her up to penetrate to the hoop. You must assess your team's strengths and employ plays that maximize those strengths. If you know your strengths and also understand how basic offensive concepts can maximize those strengths, you can develop the plays that will give your team its best chance to win.

1. Understand the Offensive Zones. When a team has the ball, the half-court area near their target basket becomes the offensive area of the court. It can be divided into seven zones—the low post, high post, pivot, point, wing, corner, and lane. The plays discussed later in this chapter will focus upon these zones. Generally, the post positions are used to bring the ball underneath the basket for a shot, while the wing and corner positions launch attacks from the outside. The point, wing, and corner zones are also together referred to as the perimeter. Take a second look at figure 2-1 on page 15, which labels each zone. Within these zones are critical areas established by different lines. The rectangular area under the basket, between the free-throw lines, is called the lane or the paint. It is also called the three-second zone. There are small squares on either side of the free-throw lines under the hoop called the blocks, and two more lines, called free-throw stripes, are painted at intervals of three feet. These markings space players who line up to rebound free throws. The free-throw or foul line is the diameter of a circle which, with the lane, is called the key (it looks sort of like a keyhole). The end of the court is called the baseline, and the mid-line of the court is also called the backcourt line. Offensive zones are often assigned numbers by the coach. Different coaches may have different terms; if so, your players will need to learn them. Language varies across the country.

2. Take the High-Percentage Shot. You've got to put the ball in the hoop! The bottom line of basketball is that the team with the most points wins. In the final analysis, scoring comes from good shooting, and good shooting comes from good shot selection.

The high-percentage shot is any shot taken with a minimum of defensive pressure, as close to the hoop as possible.

This means that you need kids who can shoot, but, more importantly, it means that you have to get your kids into a position for a high-percentage shot. The way to get that open shot is with a combination of speed, screening, faking, quickness, and a lot of passing—a lot of motion.

Each coach has her own system, a series of offensive plays within the context of an overall offensive strategy. The best strategy is usually to try to get the ball safely into the hands of the taller players underneath, or to pick off a player defending against a good shooter. The plays are designed to get all players moving in a pattern that breaks up, frustrates, and confuses the defense. The ultimate goal is to take the high-percentage shot.

When an open player catches a pass and is open and within her shooting range, especially within twelve feet of the hoop, her first thought must be to shoot. That's the name of the game: High-percentage shots must be taken quickly. Even a poor shooter has a good chance to sink a short jumper. She shouldn't hesitate. She shouldn't think! She must shoot very quickly before a defender comes on. At that range, there's not much time, only a fraction of a second. How often have you heard the fans groan when an unsure kid fails to take a short jump shot? Players must learn to think about scoring and be quick about it.

Players should be expected to take the high-percentage shot if it is available and within their range. The contrary is just as important: If the shot is not there, if the player is under great pressure, off balance, or out of range, they shouldn't take it. Players need to learn not to force it but to wait for the better opportunity.

3. Attack From the Wing. Most play patterns begin the attack toward the basket from the wing. The point position performs like a hinge on a door, feeding the ball to the wing or to a high post. The point is usually too far from the low post to get a good pass into that area. Likewise, the corner is not the optimal place to start an attack, since a player can easily get trapped there. The wing area is the staging zone for the actual attack. The Triangle offense, explained later, is the one most used at the pro level, and the wing is the primary point of attack from the triangle. The great majority of passes from the point are to the wing area, so that's where the real action starts. The wing man, usually an off guard or a shooting guard, can either make an individual move, shoot, or drive; or she

6-1. **THE ATTACK FROM THE WING**

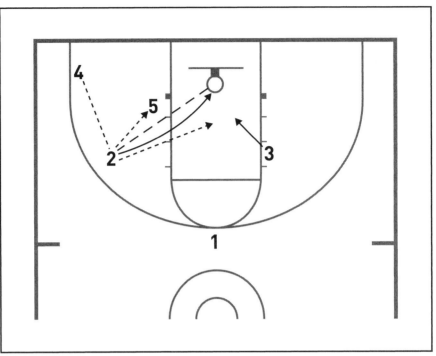

The wing positions allows for the best offensive attack. From here, the wing (#2) can pass to the corner (#4), the post (#5), or to the other wing (#3), cutting across the lane. The wing can also shoot or drive to the hoop.

can pass to the low post, to the corner, or back out to the point to reverse the ball or start another play. (See figure 6-1.)

4. Penetrate to the Post. The highest percentage shots are from underneath the basket, in the low post area. The bread-and-butter play of basketball is a pass to a big player underneath, who is posting up his defender or to a forward, "flashing," cutting back and forth under the hoop. If a team has a good, big center who knows how to post effectively and can make power moves underneath, that's about all they need. It's basketball heaven! In chapter one, I discussed the center's posting techniques. A bit later on, I will review the plays needed to get a good pass to the low post. The concept is to get the ball safely passed to a post player. (See figure 6-2.) Of course, a great dribbler can often explode through the lane, penetrating deep underneath by virtue of his own quickness. This can also be very high percentage, since this player can now shoot, dish off to the center, or

This is a bread-and-butter concept of basketball. Get the ball in to a good, big player, clear everybody else out, and let her take the ball to the hoop.

kick it back out to an open perimeter shooter. Take a look at the post-it drill for centers and low post players in chapter two, and use it frequently.

If the post player has no move available, she will pass it back to the wing to start another attack.

5. Screen Defenders and Pick and Roll. As stated before, the workhorse offensive move is the pick, or screen. The key to offensive plays is to free a player for a high-percentage shot; picks and screens do just that by blocking a defender, thus freeing up a player at least for a moment. These terms are pretty much used interchangeably anymore, although traditionally it's called a "pick" if the player to be freed has the ball, and a "screen" if the idea is to free up someone else to get the ball. The technique for both is the same. Some offenses have one or two players whose primary duty is to be a blocker, constantly seeking a screening opportunity.

The screening technique is fairly simple. A blocker runs up to the side of the defender to be screened, preferably from slightly behind so he doesn't see her coming. Timing is important. If the blocker approaches too early, the defender will have time to avoid her; if too late, the blocker may foul by running into a moving defender.

Once there, at about arm's length from the defender, the player jump stops, knees bent a bit and legs spread. She holds her elbows out, even with the opponent's chest, and pulls her hands in close to her own midsection to avoid a foul. Tell your player to brace herself, because the defender is likely to bang into her, and referees will rarely call a foul, unless it's flagrant. (See figure 6-3.)

The dribbler can set the screen up by faking one way, or v-cutting, and then driving the defender into the pick by cutting close, or nearly touching, the blocker.

I play a lot of small three-on-three games near my home, and I always look to pick the defender from the player with the ball. It's second nature. It either frees the player to dribble or shoot, or it sets up a pick and roll (explained in the next paragraph). I'm always amazed to see guys who never pick a defender. They stand still, looking around, and it never occurs to them to get involved because they never learned the concept. The pick is one of the two or three most basic offensive moves. Coach your players to always be looking to screen someone.

The pick and roll is another bread-and-butter move, and young players must learn to appreciate its value. The pick and roll is based upon the pick concept. As soon as a player picks a defender, he then pivots or rolls in the same direction that his freed-up teammate is moving, parallel with him, keeping the picked player behind him, with his hands up

6-3. **THE PICK**

Step 1: This is the most important offensive move and the most commonly made. It frees up a closely guarded teammate to dribble or shoot or sets up the pick and roll. Here, the screen is set up by the offensive player on the right.

Step 2: In this successful pick, the defender is blocked from pursuing the dribbler who now penetrates closer to the hoop.

84

6-4. THE PICK AND ROLL

Step 1: If during a pick play (see the pick in figure 6-3), the defenders switch positions to pick up the dribbler; the screener must react and begin to roll, that is, turn in a counter-clockwise spin to face the ballhandler for a possible pass.

Step 2: The roll opens the offensive receiver up for a pass and the chance for an easy lay-up.

to receive a pass. Usually, the screened defender is momentarily out of the play, so there is a two-on-one situation with the remaining defender. Often, the picker becomes free, if the player guarding him switches to cover the dribbler. If this occurs, then the picker rolls toward the basket for an easy pass and shot. (See figure 6-4.) Chapter seven will review defending the pick and when defenders should switch the players they are guarding.

Often, one offensive player will be positioned at the high post, while a guard dribbles close to her. The high-post player picks the dribbler's defender. If the pick is successful in freeing the ball handler, then the picker can roll behind the dribbler, trailing him for a possible rebound.

6. Create Constant Motion; Give and Go. Far too often in youth basketball, we see kids standing around, perhaps hopping up and down, just clogging up space. The key to offense is constant movement, with players flashing across the lane, jab stepping and two stepping in the corner, penetrating to the hoop and circling out again. The give and go perhaps best represents the benefits of quick, steady motion. It is one of the best moves in basketball, but is surprisingly underutilized. It doesn't involve a screen, just pure speed. A player simply passes to a teammate, and, *as he passes*, he explodes

6-5. **THE GIVE AND GO**

Step 1: This is a sweet move because it relies only on speed, and, if done right, results in an easy lay-up. First, the point guard passes the ball to a pivot player, who is only a relay for getting the ball back to the point guard.

Step 2: The point guard fakes right, then cuts left toward the hoop.

Step 3: The pivot player returns the ball to the point guard, who drives to the hoop for the lay-up.

forward, past his defender, and looks for a quick return pass. If done right, this move can lead to an easy lay-up. The give and go works very well at young ages, particularly for a perimeter player who passes to a high post or corner, then goes toward the basket, looking for a return pass and a lay-up. (See figure 6-5.)

7. Don't Be Too Quick to Dribble. Kids develop a bad habit of dribbling too quickly after receiving a pass. Once a player begins dribbling, he forgoes other options. Encourage your players to hesitate long enough to take a look inside, toward the hoop, for another opportunity. Obviously, if there is an opening or some space in front of the dribbler, he should quickly advance the ball. If your player is guarded, however, he shouldn't dribble, or "put the ball down," too quickly. Dribbling is only one of the initial opportunities, the others being passing and shooting. The best players look for the opportunities even before they get the ball. When underneath, a dribble can lead to a turnover, since there are many hands in a crowded space. The first instinct underneath should be a power move or a fake and a shot.

8. Pass, Pass, Pass—to an Open Space. We covered this in chapter five, but it's such an important offensive concept that it bears repeating here. The best and quickest way to move a basketball around the court and into the lanes is to pass it. Pass, pass, and pass some more! Some great teams have a rule that players not shoot until a minimum number of passes are made. This tires the defenders, opens up their defense, adds an element of confusion, and creates opportunities. Of course, the key is to pass to open space, that is, any space around a receiver in which a pass can be made safely. It's most desirable to pass to a space in the direction the receiver is heading; however, if he is guarded, that space may be very small. To ensure the opponent doesn't get the pass, players should make their pass hard and snappy, use fakes, and not broadcast their plans.

When a play is not working on one side of the floor, the reversal is a great offensive weapon. In this move, the ball is quickly passed to the point and on to the opposite wing. If done very quickly, the reversal can lead to an open high-percentage shot.

9. Move off the Ball. Many skills in basketball are hard to achieve, but the easiest of all is one of the most important: hustling. Hustle is key to basketball, and moving, even without the basketball, is what makes teams winners. It's the movement off the ball that creates possibilities for successful action on the ball. With or without the ball, a player should think about where to go.

It's hard to catch a pass when closely guarded, so a player must constantly think about how to shed her opponent. Jabbing moves, suddenly reversing direction, are great for getting free for a pass. If a player's job is to screen, where is the best spot for them to set it up, and what is the right timing? What is the ballhandler seeing? What is she thinking about? If the play breaks down, what does she need to do? Screen? Shed the defender? Screen someone else to free a teammate up for a pass? How can she help out in this situation?

Tell players they are *always* in the game and are always impacting the team, every second, for the good or for the bad.

Explain to your players that they won't get the ball passed to them if defenders are near them. Your play patterns, covered later in this chapter, will help them with their movement off the ball, when they do not personally have the ball, but they need to understand the concept. They have to find a way to get open, create open space, or move toward it.

There are three good ways to do that, individually, without the help of another teammate's screen: the jab step, the v-cut, and the circle.

Jab Step. To execute a jab step, the player takes one or two steps toward the defender and then, suddenly and quickly, stops and comes back to her original position. The defender will tend to back up a bit at first, which gets his weight going backward, off balance. Usually, the jab step will get a player open for a good second or so. It's enough.

V-Cut. This move is similar to the jab step. The player takes one or two quick steps in one direction, then suddenly changes direction. The path taken resembles the letter *V*.

The Circle. Another method for getting free of a defender is the circle. In this move, the player just revolves around the defender for a half or full circle. This confuses the defender, gets him off balance, and the player can then quickly dart out for a pass before the defender recovers.

Timing is always important. A player needs to sense when a teammate will look her way to pass and try to get open at that time. Timing will come with experience.

10. Follow the Shot; Crash the Boards. Once the shot is off, unless you instruct a player to stay back to stop a defensive fast break, the shooter and other players must follow the shot and crash the boards. About one in six rebounds will bound back toward the shooter, more if the shot is from the point, so a good follow-up move will get many of them. Offensive rebounds are usually those that bounce out a good distance, since defensive players usually have the best position for short rebounds. Most rebounds come off the opposite side of the basket from where the shot was taken, so players should position themselves on that side, moving laterally to avoid being boxed out. I will discuss rebounding more in chapter seven.

OFFENSIVE PLAY PATTERNS

"Run the Offense! Run the Offense!" If you attend a high school game you will often hear the coach exhorting the team to run the offensive play patterns chosen for the team. These are continuous motion patterns, or a set of specific plays to try to get someone open for a high percentage shot.

MOVES, PLAYS, MOTION OFFENSES, AND IMPROVISATION

To get the jargon straight, basketball has individual moves, set plays, and motion or continuous motion offenses. A move is an individual movement, such as: v-cut, jab step, pick, screen, fake, and so forth. A play involves two or more players and puts together a number of moves to achieve a specific result, such as a pick and roll, a give and go, or a scissor—all of which try to get someone free for a pass or open shot. A continuous motion offense, or pattern, is a series of plays which continue until a shot is taken.

Of course, in the real world, away from the blackboard where the Xs and Os plot out the ideal result, plays and patterns break down, and so players need to improvise, or *make something happen*. The best players can make their own plays, seizing the opportunity of the moment: seeing a defender off balance or out of position, a height mismatch, or a gap in an open lane.

However, it's important that the overall movement of the offensive players be orderly and consistent. You want to keep your players moving. Young players often get mesmerized by the action and tend to stand around and watch their teammates. Or you will see them flitting up and down, prancing about, not knowing where to go or what to do. Often they will run up to the ball carrier and just further clog up his options, since they are now too close for a pass. Patterns tell the kids where to go and what to do. It's helpful to the passer to know ahead of time where her teammates are going to be. The plays and continuous motion offenses try to do just that.

Patterns are often a series of plays designed to set players in motion by having them use screens or speed to get someone open for the high-percentage shot. If no player is open, the play continues to move players around until someone is free or until someone "makes it happen." At any time, a player may seize an opportunity. All players, while running the pattern, should look for an opportunity to score or hit an open player.

BEGINNER, INTERMEDIATE, AND ADVANCED LEVELS

Throughout this book, I have often noted differences in the various levels of play and suggested how to approach these differences. For the main part, most of what I have said in the prior chapters pertains to all ages and skill levels. Playing basketball is just a learning process that takes years. However, the differences in skill and ability between beginners and more advanced kids is quite substantial, and nowhere is the difference more profound than in trying to develop offensive plays and an overall offense for the team. So, this is a good spot to talk a bit specifically about these differences. The three levels, beginner, intermediate, and advanced, relate to the skill level of players and can therefore apply to any age. Of course, generally, for their first several years, most kids are beginners, and they slowly move on to higher skill levels.

Beginner. There is no set age when kids start playing hoops. Kids get little plastic hoops and undersized basketballs as soon as they can throw a ball. In most towns in my section of central New Jersey, organized clinics begin by about second grade. Some towns, though very few, have clinics even earlier. Some clinics combine grades to form teams. Some have teams for each grade. They will generally practice for an hour once a week and play once or twice. At first, games usually book the gym, usually a half-gym, for an hour, and they play seven to eight "quarters" of a running (clock never stops) five minutes each. Scores are not kept, and goals are few. Defense is a zone. Kids are not allowed to press until the ball is past mid-court. Traveling violations and fouls are not called at first, unless very flagrant and are slowly worked in by about fourth grade. Also, by fourth or fifth grade, the games begin to take a more regulation-type approach. There are a lot of steals, errant passes, and kids freezing over the ball. Shots are few. At first, they are two-handed chest shots, and they look like bricks thrown too hard and on a straight line with little chance of scoring.

I would say the beginner level lasts until fourth or fifth grade for most kids. The ability to learn plays is very limited, and complex continuity patterns are generally out of the question. Some large programs will take the best players onto a traveling team, and the higher skill level of these kids will allow for some basic plays. However, even in a recreation program, kids can be taught simple screens and give-and-go plays. Many coaches don't bother, focusing entirely on dribbling, passing, and shooting skills. My view is you need to try to get some offensive concepts and plays going even at the earliest levels. Just don't expect too much!

At the very least, all beginners need to learn how to screen. The perimeter players should all be encouraged to screen for each other. Tell your players, if they are close to

91

someone who just got a pass, to set a pick. Get pick crazy! Really push it in practice—it will lay the foundation for more plays later, since most plays are based on screens and picks.

Intermediate. The level of play increases substantially between the recreation clinics and the school or traveling teams. This transition usually begins by fourth or fifth grade. These traveling teams, as well as the recreation teams in sixth and seventh grades, can play at the intermediate level. There is still a wide range of ability, since some kids will demonstrate advanced skills, while others are still very much beginners but are tall enough or athletic enough to make the team. At this level, all simple plays should be taught and utilized, depending on how often you have practice. Traveling teams often get several practices a week, and so play patterns can be taught. By sixth or seventh grade, the clinic or recreation teams can begin to learn motion offenses and continuity patterns.

Advanced. Certainly by high school, and probably by eighth grade, the full range of offensive patterns can and should be employed. Kids at this level play nearly every day, and there is time to make motion offenses work. Much repetition is needed.

Given the above, we will present the offensive plays and patterns according to skill level.

BEGINNER-LEVEL PLAYS

Most practice time at this level will be devoted to basic skills, such as dribbling, passing, rebounding, and shooting. The first step in coaching team offense is to teach screens. Urge each player to look to screen for a teammate if he is closest to that teammate.

Many teams pay no further attention to running plays, and, given lack of practice time and skill level, this is quite understandable. However, you have got to start sometime. So I urge you try. A few plays can be taught to kids at the beginner level, perhaps by third grade or so, and they are all screen plays. They are the scissor, the post-interchange, and the double screen. To teach the plays, I'd number them 1, 2, and 3. If the play was to approach from the right side, they would say *Red*, and from the left, they would say *Green*. So, a scissor started by a guard on the right side would be called 1-Red, and a post-interchange from the left side would be called 2-Green. You can orally call the plays or use a signal, perhaps just with a hand or fist signaling a certain play. Start with one play, and slowly add more. I always started the kids off with a 2-1-2 offensive setup, two guards, a center in the middle—at the high post or pivot zones—and two forwards, who begin play about five feet outside of the low post blocks. The plays can also be used with a 1-2-2 set up, one point guard, two wing guards, and two forwards. (See figure 6-6.)

92

6-6. OFFENSIVE SET UP

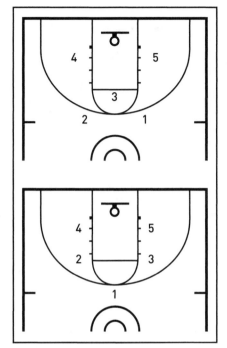

2-1-2. Used more at beginner levels, where two ball handlers are needed to advance the ball, and a tall player at high post or pivot receives passes.

1-2-2. Used at intermediate levels, where a point guard is able to initiate offenses, and patterns requiring two wing players are used.

The Scissor

Also known as a single-pivot, the Scissor is not a continuous pattern, but it is the most common three-on-three play in basketball, splitting or scissoring off the high-post. This play involves the high-post man and both guards, or a medium-pivot player with a forward and guard on the ball side of the court. The high-pivot man moves into a position in the outer half of the free-throw circle. As he reaches the position, the ball is passed to him by either guard. The pivot man moves toward the ball, catching the ball with both feet in the air and landing on both feet simultaneously and facing mid-court, his back to the basket, with well-balanced foot spread. In this manner, either foot can be the pivot foot. As he receives the ball, the guards crisscross in a scissor move in front of him, the off guard (who did not make the pass) going first. The center may give (hand off or short pass) the ball to either guard as they pass in front of him. If not, he turns to face the hoop, then may either look again to pass to one of the guards, or drive, or shoot himself. The forwards can also flash (post-interchange) underneath, creating another passing opportunity. (Post-interchange is described on pages 94–95.) The off guard circles

93

6-7. **THE SCISSOR**

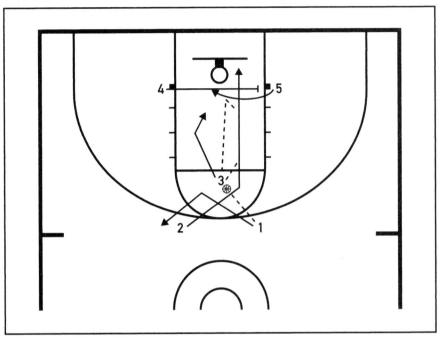

#1 passes to #3 at the high-post pivot and cuts to left of #3 for possible hand-off. #2 follows, quickly scissor-cutting by #3, also for a hand off. #1 drops back if she doesn't get the ball, and #2 cuts through lane with or without ball. #3 can hand off to either guard, or turn to shoot, or follow #2 to the hoop. She can also pass to #5, whose defender is screened by #4. If nothing works, pass out to #1 for a new play.

and quickly returns to the point for a pass back out in case the play fails or to be ready for transition defense. (See figure 6-7.) The play, as diagrammed, would be 1-Red. The Scissor can also be initiated by the off guard, #2, and this would be 1-Green. Again, the color designations worked for me at beginner levels; later on, I would just use numbers or hand signals for plays. It's useful to teach the kids that plays can be run to either side; doing this confuses the defense a bit, and that's what continuity patterns seek to do (as discussed below). With a 1-2-2 offense, the right wing would come to set the post, and the left wing would v-cut out towards the point and then cut around the post.

The Post-Interchange

We talked earlier about having players get the ball to the wing and having the wing try to pass it to the big player posting up underneath. A good play to accomplish this has two big players line up on the opposite low-post blocks and then switch positions. (See figure 6-8.) The player moving away from the ball moves first, screening the oncoming defender who is guarding the other big player. This second player is now flashing across the lane toward the middle and is free to receive a pass underneath. She should, in the best case, get the ball just after passing the screen. The screening player should always position herself closer to the baseline, so the other player can get outside for the pass. We called this play number 2, so the play in the figure would be called 2-Green. It can also be called from the right wing, in which case, it would be called 2-Red.

This play is diagrammed for a 1-2-2, but, as with all three plays, can be modified for a 2-1-2 by having the pivot player receive the first pass and then turn and pass underneath.

6–8. POST-INTERCHANGE

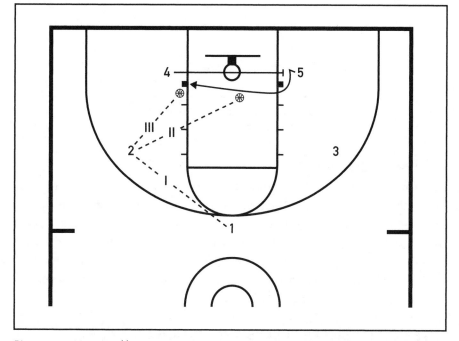

Play starts with a pass (i) to wing #2. As ball is being passed, #4 flashes to set a screen for #5, who cuts around, looking for a pass from #2. If no quick pass (ii), #5 sets up a low post and looks for that pass (iii). The concept here is to interchange these tall players back and forth to get free for an easy shot.

6-9. **DOUBLE SCREEN**

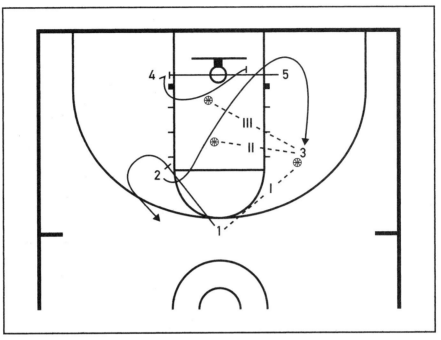

#1 passes (i) to #3 and then proceeds to screen for #2. #3 passes (ii) to #2, shuffling through the lane, or to #4, cutting off #5's screen, trailing #2.

The Double Screen

A nice play I've tried in clinic basketball has two screens set, one for the off guard and one for the weak side forward. The point guard passes to a wing shooting guard. (See figure 6-9.) Then the point guard quickly darts to the high post and picks the player defending the off guard. The off guard cuts around the screen into the lane, looking for a pass. The wing can either shoot, drive, pass to the off guard, or pass to the weak side forward—cutting around her screen. Figure 6-9 shows the play attacking from the right wing, so the call would be 3-Red.

INTERMEDIATE-LEVEL PLAYS AND MOTION OFFENSES

At fifth through seventh grades, the players should already be familiar with basic screens and give-and-go plays. If they aren't yet familiar with these plays, start them there. After those concepts are working, start the players on one of the following patterns: the McShuffle or the wheel pattern. After they have mastered one, start with the next. The

McShuffle builds more upon the perimeter players, whereas the wheel focuses more on getting the ball into the post, to the bigger players. Start with the one which best utilizes your team's strength.

At this level, you will have difficulty using one pattern, let alone two. There are two others I've used against the zone called the clock and the stack zone buster, which you may wish to consider also.

The McShuffle

The regular version of the Shuffle, based largely on the scissor-cut concept, is probably one of the oldest and most widely used play patterns in basketball. I learned it as a kid, and I've seen it used many times since. The shuffle is presented for advanced-level play, later in this chapter. I adapted a version of the shuffle for the middle-school level of play, since the regular version takes tall players too far away from the lane, and that can be a problem at this level. I call it the McShuffle. The diagram in figure 6-10 describes each step, and I refer you to it to learn the pattern, so I don't need to repeat

6-10. THE MCSHUFFLE

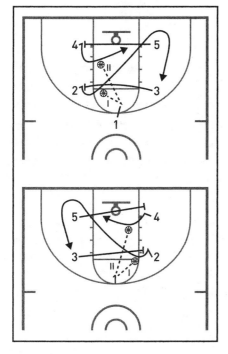

First shuffle: #2 v-cuts around the high post screen set by #3, as the screen is set (timing!), #5 clears out and sets a screen for #4. #2 gets pass (i) from #1 and drives to shoot or to dish off to #4 coming off #5's screen. If no pass to #2, #1 looks to pass (ii) to #4, trailing #2.

Reshuffle: If nothing was open, the players are now in position for another McShuffle, this time from the other side, with #3 and #5 respectively setting screens.

the moves here. Basically, the idea is for the team to penetrate strongly up the middle, first with a wing player, freed up by a screen or a "rub cut," and then by a forward flashing across the lane behind that wing player. If this doesn't work, players move to positions from which the McShuffle can be run again from the other side. This pattern also works better against the zone defenses regularly employed at this level, since it overloads each side alternatively. The McShuffle is called a continuous motion pattern, since it can be continuously run until a shot is taken.

The players must all know how to move from position to position. It seems like a lot to know, but that's what practice is for. The point is that, during the shuffle, all players are in constant motion all over the floor, creating opportunities. Usually the pattern needs to be run only once or twice before a good shooting opportunity is created, or before a player tries to make something happen. The shuffle is called a continuity pattern because if it fails, the team is already set up to run it the other way.

In teaching this pattern, have the kids walk though it. Try one play with a pass to the #2 guard cutting off the high post, then try one with the pass to the secondary player, the flashing forward trailing #2. Finally, try one with no pass, and simply start the shuffle from the left side. Have the players move slowly at first. Walk them through the steps. Repeat it many times—it will eventually sink in!

The Wheel Pattern

Another nice offense against a zone is a wheel-type motion, which not only overloads the Zone, but keeps everyone in motion. (See figure 6-11.) The diagram will walk you through it. This pattern basically starts the attack from the wing. The first play (unless the wing sees an opportunity to drive or shoot) is a give and go with the corner player. If no pass is made, the weak-side forward flashes off a screen to get a low-post pass. Players constantly rotate, *turning the wheel*, to fill vacated positions, and, if nothing works, the floor is set up for a wheel the other way.

Give, Go, and Wheel

A nice variation of the wheel concept for intermediate players, useful against any defense, involves a series of possible give-and-go moves. Give-and-go plays work well from the point position using a wing or from the wing using a corner player. If a give and go is not executed, then the players spin the wheel to fill in gaps vacated by the cutting player and try again. (See figure 6-12 on page 100.)

6-11. WHEEL PATTERN

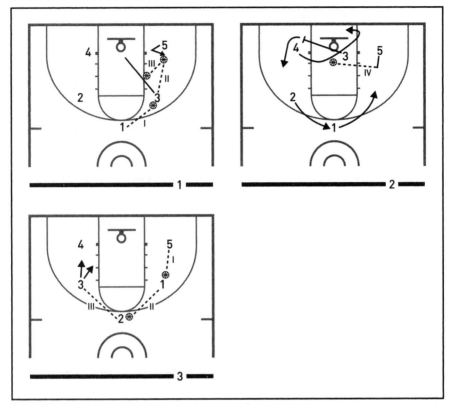

1. #1 passes (i) to #3, who looks to shoot or drive. #5 v-cuts to corner. If #3 can't make a move, #3 passes (ii) to the corner and looks for a give and go (iii). As soon as #3 moves toward the hoop, #2 and #1 begin to turn the wheel, floating to the right.

2. If #5 doesn't get the ball to #3, then #3 picks for #4, who flashes across the lane for pass (iv). If no pass, then the wheel turns, with #3 to the left wing and #4 circling back to his original low post.

3. If nothing was open, players reverse quickly, #5 to #1 to #2 to #3 to start over again, working the wheel on the other side.

6–12. **GIVE, GO, AND WHEEL**

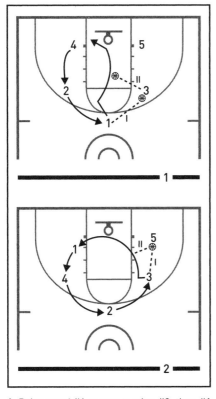

6–13. **THE CLOCK OFFENSIVE**

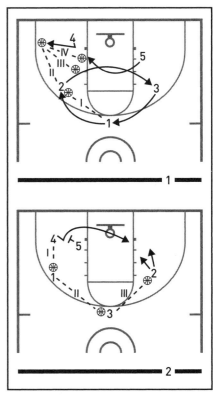

1. Point guard #1 passes to wing #3, then #1 V-cuts for a give and go toward the hoop. If #3 can't pass back to #1, #1 replaces #4, as #4 and #2 turn the wheel counterclockwise to reestablish the 1-2-2.

2. #3 still has the ball. She passes to #5, then v-cuts for a give and go. If #5 can't get her the ball, then the players again turn the wheel. #5 can make a move, such as passing to #2 for another give and go or get the ball out to the top of the key for another play.

1. #1 passes (i) to #2, who passes (ii) to #4. #2 cuts across lane for a give and go (iii) from #4. If no pass back to #3, then #1, #2, and #3 rotate clockwise to each others' spots. #5 trails #3, looking for a low-post pass (iv) from #4, and #4 also looks to drive baseline or shoot.

2. If nothing happens, then #4 reverses quickly to #1, then to #3, then to #2 in right wing. #5 sets up a screen for #4, who runs to low post. #3 looks to shoot or drive off the reversal, or to pass to #4 if defender comes out.

The Clock Offense

A great offense pattern against the zone is the clock, so-called because of the clockwise or counterclockwise movement of the perimeter players. Zone offenses are characterized by rapid, outside passing to open up the defensive zone's gaps, plays to

100

overload players on one side to get someone free, and sudden quick reversals to the other side when the defense tries to double-team or add defenders to the overloaded side. (See figure 6-13.)

In the Clock, the point guard passes to a wing, who passes into the corner. All three perimeter players start moving clockwise to replace each other's position. The corner forward hits the wing, cutting to the lane on a give and go, or hits the low post trailing the wing.

If the pass to either player was not open, then the forward reverses by quickly passing out to the point guard, who in turn quickly passes to the off guard and then on to the opposite wing. Quick passing is paramount, so the wing may be now be open for a drive or an unobstructed shot. The corner then cuts across the lane off the center's screen to the other low post and looks for a pass from the forward, particularly if the baseline defender goes after that forward.

6-14. THE STACK-ZONE BUSTER

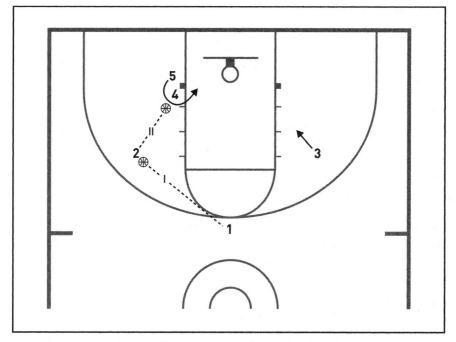

#1 passes to wing #2. #5 circles #4, looking for pass. If no good, #2 can pass to #4 who trails #5. #5 can reverse around #4 the other way or come out and pick for #2.

The Stack Zone Buster

This is another great pattern that overloads the zone with two players on one side of the lane, in a low- to mid-post position. The forward player is a stable pick for the center to rub, circle, and screen against. The players get the ball into the wing and look for an opportunity to get a pass to the center. (See figure 6-14 on page 101.)

ADVANCED-LEVEL OFFENSES

Certainly by high school, and maybe even before, players should at least be familiar with all fundamentals, moves, plays, and some motion and continuity offenses. If your players are not at this level, you have to start where the prior coaches left off. Hopefully, you will be able to introduce multiple continuity patterns and refine the ones you will employ. The McShuffle and Wheel patterns are two very good continuity patterns. I'll describe three more popular ones here: the shuffle, the flex, and the pro triangle offense. These are generally offenses for use against man-to-man defense.

6–15. THE SHUFFLE

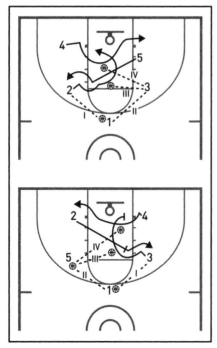

First shuffle: #2 passes (i) to #1 as #5 comes out to set a screen for #2. As #1 passes (ii) to #3, #2 rub-cuts around the high-post screen and looks for pass (iii) from #3. #5 floats to the wing. If #2 gets no pass, he circles to screen for #4, who cuts through the lane. If no pass, #4 goes to #5's low post area.

Reshuffle: Floor is now set up to run the shuffle the other way, with #2 screening for #3, and #4 looking to trail. #3 begins the reversal to #1, then to #5 in the wing to start the attack from the left side.

The Shuffle

I presented my intermediate variation above, the McShuffle. The regular shuffle is similar, but it varies in that one of the two tall players is pulled out to the high post and then to the point. It's okay if your players are more equal in ability, and you don't have a dominant big person. In a man-to-man defense, the shuffle will draw the opponents' big players outside. It's an offense for smaller, quick teams. Figure 6-15 on page 102 walks you through the motion.

The Flex

This offense relies mainly upon picks and screens and usually sets at least two screens at a time. It's very popular, and simple to run. Players need to understand the concept that they alternate getting and giving a pick. See figure 6-16 for the play pattern and review it carefully. The play focuses on getting the ball underneath to the big players, who get a screen, opening them for a baseline drive to the hoop. If the first pick is not productive, then the play crosses to the other side, and a forward from that side gets a pick for a baseline drive.

6–16. THE FLEX OFFENSE

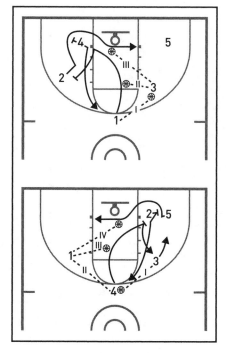

Flex left. #1 passes to wing #3, and heads through lane for a give and go (II) or, if no pass, to screen for #4. #2 cuts around #4's screen, looking for a pass underneath (III). After setting the screen, #4 cuts around #1's screen and heads to the point. #1 floats back to wing, and #3 looks for another opportunity. Otherwise reverse.

Flex right. Offense is now set up for a flex right. #3 reverses (i) to #4, who passes (ii) quickly to #1. Then players flex, #4 flashes through lane for a pass (iii) or to set a screen for #2. #2 screens for #5 who looks for a pass (iv) from #1, then #3 cuts around #4's screen to the point. #2 floats to the corner.

The Triangle

Probably the dominant professional offense of the past fifteen years is the triangle offense. It relies much less upon screens or motion, as do the flex and shuffle offenses. The Triangle relies more upon proper floor spacing, passing, cutting, and individual initiative. The Triangle creates opportunities within a framework which spreads and isolates the defense. This framework includes a basic sideline triangle and an adjoining triangle formed by the two weak side players. The offense focuses on low-post play, and, by spreading out the defense, achieves numerous one-on-one opportunities, especially in the low post. Since this offense is generally employed at more advanced levels, I won't explore it in detail here. A fair amount of literature is available on the Internet. (See figure 6-17.) Basically, a sideline triangle forms between the corner, wing, and low

6-17. **THE TRIANGLE OFFENSE**

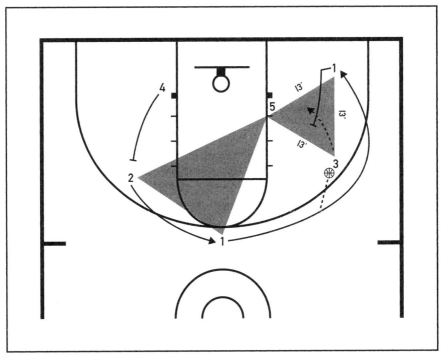

Floor position and distance is the key. #1 circles to the corner after passing to #3 and sets up a triangle with #3 and #5, with legs about 13 feet apart. #2 floats to point and #4 shifts to wing. #2 and #4 also set themselves in a slightly larger triangle. #3 passes in to #5, who makes a low-post move. If no good, he passes back out to #1 or #3. They can pick for each other, or reverse quickly to #2 and on to #4 for a shot or drive, or pass back to the triangle.

post, with sides about twelve to fifteen feet long at the youth and high-school level of play. The remaining two players cover the point and weak-side high post, forming an adjoining triangle. This triangle can quickly switch play to the weak side, if needed, particularly if a double-team forms around the post and the weak side opens up. While the focus is to get low-post action, the wing and corner can pick, give and go, or scissor cut with the low post.

OFFENSIVE PATTERNS: MAN-TO-MAN OR ZONE?

The selection of an offensive play or pattern should vary, depending on the type of defense used by the opponent. In a man-to-man defense, each defender is responsible for defending a specific player, usually one of similar size, so the offense must use picks and screens to free up players. In a zone defense, defenders are assigned to defend an area (a zone), and any opponent coming into their area is their responsibility. Of course, if no opponent comes into their area, the defending players must help out in any adjoining area that has an overload of opponents. Zones are vulnerable to overloading one area of the court with more offensive players. Zones also create opportunities for the offense to mismatch players.

Motion patterns and plays generally using screens, such as the give and go, pick and roll, and jab steps, work better against man-to-man defense, but may be used against zone defenses as well. Players need to move through the gaps between defenders. However, it is tough to get inside against a zone, and so many of these plays are effective only out in the perimeter areas. As we will discuss later, the zone is sometimes banned in youth basketball, so that the kids learn how to play defense. It's banned in the pros, too, in order to promote more action under the hoop. However, zones are used heavily and are easy for kids to learn because they are so simple. Zones are also easy to coach.

A zone forces outside shooting because, essentially, defensive players bunch up around the lane and clog it up! This defense allows defenders to front the big, offensive players underneath and deny passes to them. It also makes it difficult for offensive players to drive into the congestion of defenders.

Cutting into the lane and overloading gaps of the zone is one way to attack the it. This technique requires a good, hard passer to thread the needle with crisp passes. Post-interchange or stacking plays also work well against a zone. The offense can try to overload a zone to one side, with two offensive players in an area guarded by only one defender; the clock offense does this. The idea behind busting a zone is for the players to get set up quickly, perform quick snappy perimeter passing to open up the zone, overload one area and attack, or reverse quickly and attack.

105

At advanced levels, your players should have enough skill to adapt plays to various zones. Take a look at figure 7-10, in chapter seven, which depicts various zone defenses. The 1-2-2 zone is weak in the middle and thus vulnerable to a 2-1-2 offense and to plays like McShuffle, shuffle, and flex that attack the middle. The 2-1-2 is probably the most balanced zone defense and is the most utilized. It is weak in the wings, so use a 1-2-2 and a wheel-type offense, which uses the wing area. The 1-3-1 zone is weak underneath, and the flex offense and stack-zone pattern attack underneath from a 1-2-2 offense. Finally, a 2-3 zone opens up the high post and plays, such as the shuffle, which attack the middle from a 1-2-2 offense.

FAST BREAK

This offensive play starts after a steal or defensive rebound. (See figure 6-18.) The rebounder turns and immediately passes to an outlet player on the sidelines. The key is for a guard to always be at the outlet or wing position. The guard on the side of the court with the ball action usually has the responsibility to head to the same spot on every rebound and be ready for the outlet pass.

As the ball is passed to the outlet, the point guard in the center lane and the player closest to the far sideline head to the other two fast break lanes; one lane is down the middle, and the other two are on opposite sides of the court. The outlet breaks upcourt looking to pass quickly to his teammate in the center lane. The ballhandler drives up mid-court and looks to pass to either of the sideline breakers as they move to the hoop. The original rebounder and the other player near the basket head toward the other end to help out, possibly rebounding after the fast break or defending in case the ball is turned over to the other team. After a steal, the same concept applies: The three perimeter players move to the nearest lane, looking to get the ball quickly to the center lane. This play requires speed, endurance, speed dribbling, and the ability to make a lay-up at full throttle. A good fast-break team, especially one with good speed, is tough to stop and can be very dominating. If your team comes up against one, have two players always hang back a bit in the point mid-court area to pick it up, slow the fast break down down, and force the opponents to play regular half-court offense.

The classic fast break has the rebounder (#5) passing to outlet (#3), who in turn passes to ▶ midcourt (#1). #1 drives down the middle as the two wide players (#2 and #3) streak up the sideline. All three angle toward the hoop. The remaining two players, #4 and #5, trail the play.

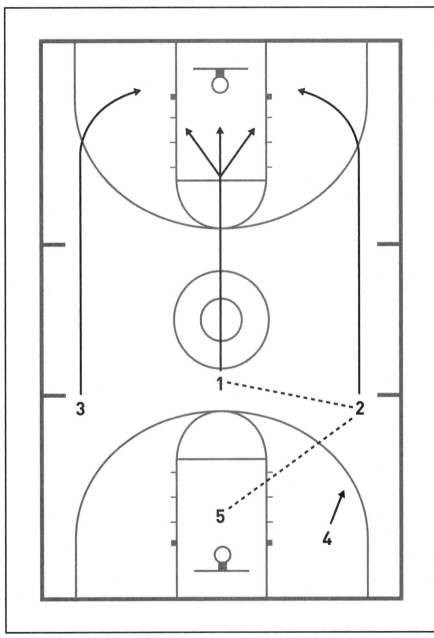

06

INBOUNDS PLAY

Each team needs a few out-of-bounds plays for getting possession of the ball when defense is pressing. One or two are needed for players to use when they inbound under the opponent's basket, one for inbounding at mid-court, and one for inbounding under

6-19. INBOUNDING PLAYS

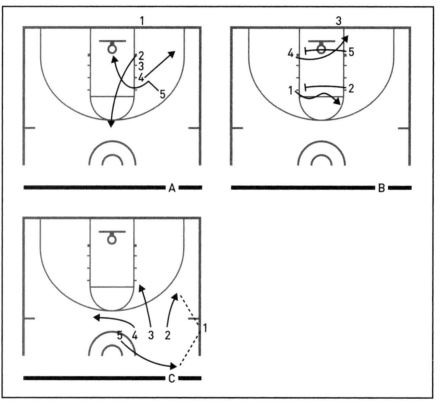

A. Stack Inbound. Under players' own hoop inbound: As #1 taps the ball, #5 cuts off #4 toward the hoop, tapping #4's back. Upon feeling this tap, #4 steps to the right for a pass. #2 rushes to the top of the key for a deep pass, in case #4 and #5 are guarded. #1 passes or fakes to #5, then looks to #4 or to stationary #3. If nothing works, look to dump out to #2.

B. Box Inbound. Players on right side both screen for players on left side. An alternative is to have one post player screen for a high-post player, #4 for #1, and a high-post screen for low post, #2 for #5.

C. Sideline Inbound. #2 cuts toward the corner, #3 heads toward the lane, #4 heads away from the ball, and #5 moves toward the ball, backcourt if necessary. All defenders are spread out. #5 is primary receiver, #2 is next.

108

the team's own basket. Figures 6-19A, 6-19B, and 6-19C suggest three patterns which can be used for any inbounds situation. The ones suggested work well for inbounding from side-court, as well as for underneath.

Inbound and Break the Press

Sometimes defenders will closely guard the inbound pass after a basket is scored. This is called a press, or full-court press. As noted earlier, the press is often prohibited in youth basketball, before about fifth or sixth grade.

Remember what I said earlier about the importance of dribbling? If you have a good ballhandler, she can break a press just by dribbling around defenders. Have your players inbound to her and get everyone else out of the way. If she needs more help,

6-20. INBOUND AND BREAK THE PRESS

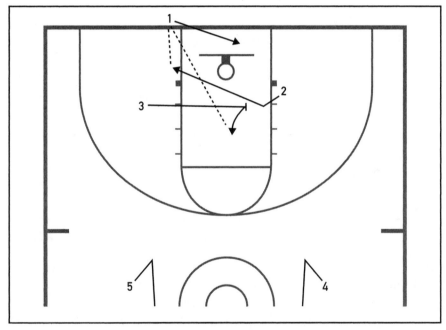

After opponent's basket with full-court press defense: #1 has ball out-of-bounds. #4 and #5 fake toward the ball and then head up court to draw their men away; however #5, a big player, loops back to backcourt to help out if needed. #3 screens for #2, who fakes left and cuts to #1 for the ball. #1 can also pass to #3, who rolls off the screen upcourt. #1 gets open for a pass back if the receiver, #2 or #3, gets double-covered. #5 is open for a high pass in an emergency.

get your biggest player with good hands and some dribbling ability to mid-court. There are only ten seconds allowed get the ball past the mid-court line, and a big player can usually catch a high pass at mid-court if time is running out.

Figure 6-20 on page 109 provides a good inbound play to break the press. The two best dribblers simultaneously screen and then release each other's defenders, hoping at least one of them gets free for the inbound. If the inbounder is pressured, she is free to run along the baseline for an open pass, but only five seconds are allotted. Whoever gets the ball heads upcourt. Meanwhile, a big player positions herself near mid-court to help if needed.

CENTER TAP

A center tap occurs at the beginning of the game, as well as any time officials disagree or when play is stopped for injury. At the beginning of the game, two players face each other at center court; in other situations, they stand at the center of the foul line closest to where play was stopped. The other players position themselves outside of the circle on the floor. The referee throws the ball straight up between the two players in the middle, and they each endeavor to tap the ball to a teammate.

If you are sure your player can win the tap, then use the play in figure 6-21A. Have your center tap directly to a guard, and have him pass to one of two other players who immediately head towards the basket. If you are unsure or expect your center to lose the tap, you can't afford to send players toward the offensive basket. Instead, send one immediately to the defensive basket, and have the other players cover probable receivers. (See figure 6-21B.)

OFFENSIVE DRILLS

Here are some drills and variations that you can simplify, as needed, and add difficulty to as the players mature.

Walk-Throughs. Whatever play patterns you choose must be drilled until they are second nature. Hand out diagrams and talk the players through the moves. It's far easier for your players to understand a play if they see it first. Next, walk your team through the pattern several times, slowly adding light defense, then start having them run the pattern against full pressure. Note that a kid who may be a bit less skilled overall becomes more valuable if he can run the pattern well. Some kids are very coachable in this regard. Don't ignore the value of those who regularly do just what they are told.

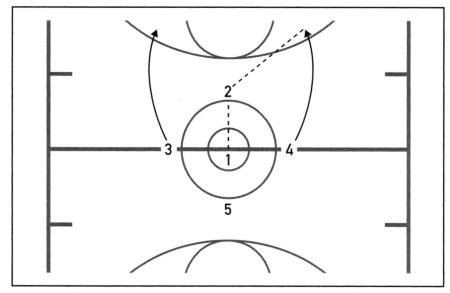

A. If sure you can win the tap: #1 taps forward to #2, #3 and #4 cut toward the basket for a quick pass from #2. #5 stays back to defend.

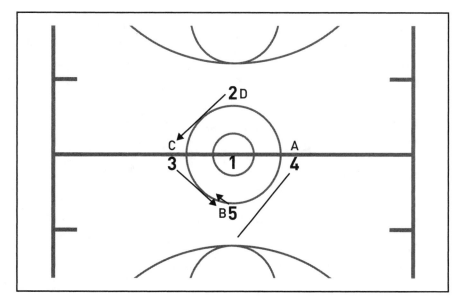

B. If unsure you can win or sure you will lose the tap: #3 and #5 knife to the probable forward receiver. #4 heads toward defensive basket. #2 knifes toward C, the other probable receiver. Players don't move until ball is thrown.

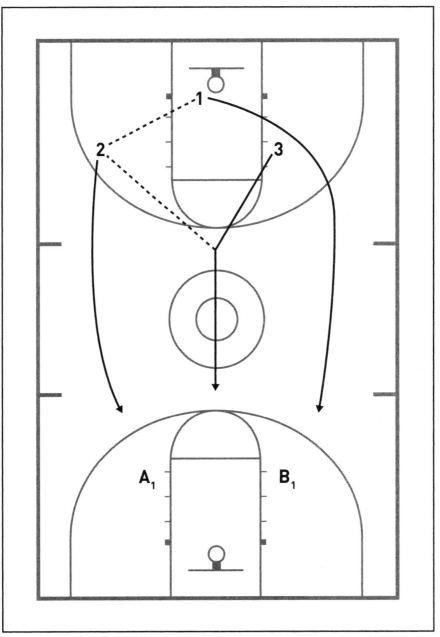

Three-on-Two-on-One Drill. One of the most popular drills for many years, the three-on-two-on-one, is fun and is great for getting a team in shape. It practices a running fast-break game and incorporates shooting, defense, rebounding, and speed dribbling. For young beginners, you may wish to start with just the three-on-two drill. After the three players make a basket or lose the ball, bring in five new players. For more experienced players, the drill can flow directly into the two-on-one. Whoever among the three players lost the ball, missed, or made the shot must then defend against the two previous defenders, while they drive down the court to try and score. While the two-on-one is in progress, two new defenders come on the floor and set up. Once the

6-23. CRISSCROSS DRILL

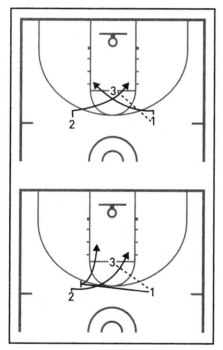

#1 passes to the pivot #3 and cuts off his left hip. #2 follows, faking right and then cutting off #3's right hip. #3 hands off to either guard to turn to shoot or drive.

Roll variation: #1 passes to #3 and then screens #2's man. #2 fakes left, then cuts off #3's right hip. #1 rolls clockwise, pivoting off right foot. #3 can pass to either guard, or turn to drive or shoot.

◀ #1 stands under the hoop and banks the ball off the board to simulate a rebound. She yells "Ball!" when she gets the rebound and passes it to outlet #2. #3 runs to midcourt to get the ball from #2, and #1 and #2 head down the sideline. They try to score against defenders A and B. Beginners can stop here and bring on a new crew. Otherwise, bring in new players after a rebound, steal, lost ball, or score. A or B grabs the ball and, without inbounding, immediately heads the other way to score.

113

two-on-one is completed by a rebound or score, those same three players start the fast break again against the two new defenders. (See figure 6-22 on page 112.) The drill I offer is a continuous drill, and it is much better when learned by the team.

Crisscross Drill. I include two crisscross drills here: a simple crisscross off a pivot man and a screen, crisscross, and roll. After the players know the pattern, you may add some defenders. (See figure 6-23 on page 113.)

Stop, Pivot, Go Drill. Footwork drills are essential. This one is a favorite of mine because the pivot and spin are fundamental foot skills which greatly expand a player's ability to navigate the floor through defensive traffic. The stop, pivot, go drill allows players to practice footwork without pressure. By running directly at a defender, the offensive player gets

6-24. **STOP, PIVOT, AND GO DRILL**

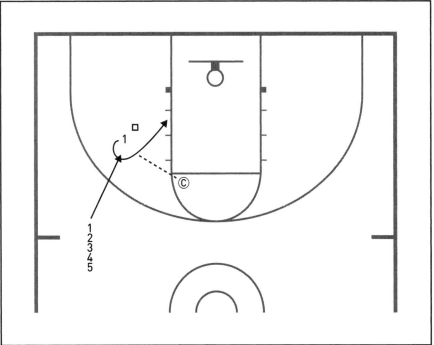

Place a chair or dummy defender at the wing area. Players line up along the sideline. First player runs at the chair, jump stops, then pivots off the inside foot counterclockwise (from the left side of the court), facing the coach or a guard in the key, who then passes the ball for a lay-up. Have players do this from both sides. You can form two lines to run it alternatively from each side.

her to lean back a bit. The jump-stop and spin movement depicted in figure 6-24 allows the offensive player to present a clear target for a pass by spinning to face the passer.

Reverse Cut Drill. Another good footwork drill is the reverse cut. Here, the player double-fakes the defender, first with a body fake, then with a jab step, before darting into the lane. (See figure 6-25.)

'Round-the-World Drill. A very popular drill. Three or four players line up along each sideline, evenly spaced. One player runs down one side, passing give and go to each teammate and eventually shooting a lay-up, before heading down the other side, repeating the drill. Then another player takes a turn, and the first player replaces someone in line. (See figure 6-26 on page 116.)

6–25. **REVERSE CUT DRILLS**

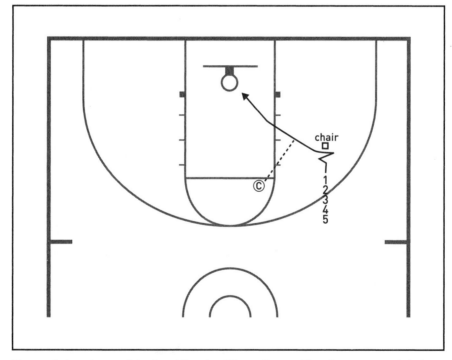

Place a chair or dummy defender at the wing. Players line up. First player runs at chair, jump stops, makes a fake to the left, pushes off with the left foot for a short step to the right, and then takes a large step with the left foot driving past the defender, stretching for a pass. The coach or guard in the key passes the ball for a lay-up.

115

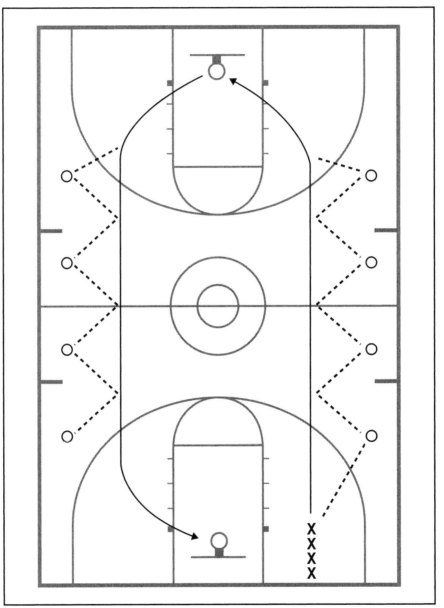

A great team drill! Space four players along each sideline. The remaining players dribble down each side, passing back and forth to each successive teammate, then shoot, get the rebound, and proceed down other side. Have several balls going at a time. Rotate players into the line, or switch groups, depending on how many players you have. Try to get everyone on the floor.

DEFENSE AND REBOUNDING   07

Some of the images most associated with basketball are those of Michael Jordan twisting high in the air for a reverse slam dunk or Larry Bird popping in a three-pointer. However, more and more, we herald the great rebounding of a Ben Wallace, or a Dikembe Mutombo rejecting an attempted shot, or the quick hands of Ron Artest stealing passes.

It's called defense. You need to make a serious commitment to its importance and communicate it to your players. Kids often play poorly on defense: They fail to stay between their opponent and the hoop, allow players to drive around them, are easily faked out, and miss opportunities to steal the ball by not being alert. These are the four primary defensive weaknesses, so make sure your players understand them. Parents can reiterate the idea at home.

DEFENSE IS A STATE OF MIND

Anyone can be a good defensive player. It's much easier to do things without the ball than with it. The ball slows a player down. Defense is mainly a matter of desire, hustle, agility, energy, and endurance. Sure there are skills, and we'll discuss them, but defense is mainly a state of mind: Great defenders play as though the opponent has no right to the ball, whatsoever. Tell your kids they will get more playing time if they become good at defense, and that they can become good just by wanting to!

A good defensive team seems frantic to get the ball back. A good defensive player always knows where the ball is and always looks for a chance to get her hands on it. You need to instill a bit of fury into the team when they are playing defense. The message here is oral, and you need to communicate it over and over—*get excited on defense!*

If a player gets the message and becomes ball-crazy on the floor, it could be the beginning of an excellent ball player. The amount of playing time a kid gets is usually closely associated with her all-around ability to contribute. Coaches know they will have only a couple of players who can score, and they need players who can do other things.

117

A poor defensive player is a liability to the team. A coach can give playing time to poor offensive players—they can be hidden better. But nothing upsets coaches more than a poor defensive effort.

THE TOP TEN DEFENSIVE CONCEPTS

There are a number of defensive concepts that need to be impressed upon young players. Remember, defense is mainly attitude, and, if your player gets that idea, it will help him draw that attitude from within.

1. Defense Begins with Transition Play: Hustle Back and Set Up. You can't play defense on the wrong end of the court. Players must get back to their defensive post or assignment very quickly when the other team gets the ball. It's one thing to see a tired player come upcourt slowly on offense. It's entirely another for a player to react slowly on defense. Players who do this will soon find themselves on the bench. Getting back on defense is the time to sprint. Many games are lost in this transitional part of the game. Opposing teams see this weakness and quickly capitalize on it with fast breaks.

When a player is beaten by a ballhandler, he must turn and run down court, try to get in front of the ballhandler, and set up to defend again. Remember, a defender can almost always outrun a dribbler. The common error is for a player to go directly for the ball, reaching or bumping the dribbler, which often results in a foul. A player must hustle back and set up for defensive play. He should catch the offensive player first, then pivot and defend.

Catch-Up Drill. Put the defender on the mid-court line, facing away from opponent's basket. Have a player with the ball stand next to her. The offensive player starts to dribble toward the hoop to shoot, and the defender turns and chases, trying to catch up and disrupt the shot, but she must be careful not to foul.

2. Triple-Threat Stance. The most important fundamental in most sports is proper form. It is the foundation onto which a player adds his individual ability. Good form will position a player to execute a move. It maximizes quickness, the ability to react, and the balance needed to launch a good shot. A proper stance is the easiest thing to coach and is achieved by constant drilling and repetition. However, in the heat of play or when a player is tired, a poorly laid foundation of form is the first thing to fall apart.

We've already covered the triple-threat offensive position. Well, there is also a triple-threat defensive position, which coaches also call the "basketball position." In

7-1. TRIPLE-THREAT DEFENSE

The triple-threat defense provides a position from which a defender can move forward, right or left, and defend against a shot, pass, or dribble.

this defensive position, a player lines up one long step from the person with the ball, just far enough so the defender can reach out and touch the opponent's chest. The triple-threat requires the legs to be spread and the weight to be balanced on the balls of the feet. The body is low in a crouch, knees bent, waist partially bent. The head is up, always. Hands are out in front of the body, spread outside shoulder width. Palms are in or up; this is important to reduce fouls. Referees tend to call the downward hand motion a foul, but not an upward motion.

The triple-threat posture allows the defender to move forward, sideways, or vertically to stop a dribble, a pass, or a shot. Triple-threat is simply the position that best allows the player to make any one of those three moves in a split second.

A central concept to good defensive play is to stay low in the triple-threat position, below the opponent. How low? The player's head should be below the opponent's chin. If the opponent lowers his head to drive, the defensive player should get even lower. The low position allows a defender to stay fairly close, about a step or arm's length away. She should stay close enough that, if the opponent holds the ball in front of himself, she can knock it from his hands. Low posture allows for quick moves and reactions. It makes the body wider and gets the hands closer to the ball. It allows the defender to better see the ball. Think pressure! Think intimidation! As the ball moves, the defender *slides* with it, using quick choppy steps.

119

Slide Drill. Line players up in three lines. Have them get into a defensive triple-threat stance. The coach motions with her hand, back and forth, emulating the direction of the ball. Players slide their feet across, left or right, trying to stay with the coach's hand movements, as if an opponent is moving left or right. It is important for a player not to cross his feet (i.e., if he is moving right, he should bring his left foot to his right foot, then move his right foot out to the right). He should never cross one foot over the other.

Have your players do this drill each way ten times, for about five to eight steps.

Fast-Foot Drill. Have players get into the triple-threat defensive stance and raise and lower their feet off the ground about four inches very rapidly for about thirty to forty-five seconds. This drill develops foot speed that is critical in getting to and keeping a good position while defending.

3. Apply Great Pressure: Threaten, Dog, Trap, Smother. This is the heart of a good defense—upsetting the player with the ball in every possible way. Players should use flailing arms, shaking hand movements, grunts, groans, anything that works to distract the opponent. Just don't let them foul! Defensive players should force shooters to alter their position, timing, release, or the arc of their shot.

Another way a player can force something to happen is to fake an attack on the ball. A player doesn't need the ball to fake. A defensive player can and should fake body movements, pretending to charge the ballhandler, to get him to commit himself to a move. It all serves to confuse the opposition. I've even heard some defensive players talk to the player they are guarding, to get him riled up, to get him thinking too much about what he is doing. I don't encourage this, it is unsportsmanlike. But players should be encouraged to talk with their bodies, and the message to be sent is pure disruption.

There are basically four types of one-on-one defense away from the basket. The first, which I'll call *threaten,* is used when the opponent receives a pass but has not yet started dribbling because he is deciding what to do. The defensive player sets into a triple-threat, a step away with her hands up, threatening attacks with short jab steps. Holding hands up high prevents long, high passes and distracts the offense. However, players tend to want to play with their hands at their sides or out front; it feels more comfortable. I like to say hands should be busy. When a player is guarding one on one, she should have one hand up in the shooting lane and the other out in a passing lane, or as near to the ball as possible. The offensive player can dribble, shoot, or pass; so, in defense, players try to put pressure on two of these three actions.

The next phase of defense starts when the offensive player begins to dribble. Now the defender slide-steps with the opponent's action, *dogging* the player, cutting him off, forcing him wide. (See figure 7-2.) Finally, when a player stops dribbling and picks up the ball, he is easy prey. The defender's first instinct should be to *smother* the player, get all over him, arms flailing to distract or smack the ball away.

The *trap* is a great defensive weapon. It involves two defenders surrounding a dribbler as soon as she stops dribbling, particularly when near a sideline, and definitely when in any one of the four corners. When the dribbler is in the corner, the second defender comes in right away, particularly if the dribbler looks as though she can't get a pass off immediately. Of course, if the player is in the act of or preparing to pass, the trap won't work. This play is usually used against a short player or one who is not a good ballhandler. A well-executed trap will often force an errant pass, result in a steal, or—if the ball handler can't execute a pass in five seconds—the defense being awarded the ball. (See figure 7-3.)

7–2. **PRESSURE**

Defense is about intimidation through physical presence and through pressure from a low and stable, triple-threat defensive stance.

7–3. **THE TRAP**

Anytime two defenders can trap a dribbler, the odds for a turnover increase. Here the defenders put their inside feet side by side to block the center and use their other feet to close off the baseline.

Smother Drill. Have a player dribble the ball, then stop. As soon as he stops, the defender comes in to smother. The player with the ball pivots, trying to pass to the coach, who is standing stationary fifteen feet away. Don't allow fouls, but encourage fierce defense. Make sure players know it's for everybody's good, so they don't get frustrated.

4. Keep the Action Wide, Away From the Lane. This advice just makes common sense. The lane or "paint" area—the low and high posts—is where high-percentage shots are taken. The defense always wants to deny access into this prized area, whether to a dribbler or a passer. Defensive players should force the play to stay wide, on either side, along the perimeter or sideline.

The lowest percentage shots are those taken from the corners. These shots are long, and there is no backboard to afford perspective or to give a lucky bank to an errant shot. Your players should force the ball into the corner if at all possible. Also, the corners can be a natural place to trap an offensive player, eliminating options and allowing the defense to bottle up and really frustrate the player. It is important, however, to protect against a baseline drive and to force the ball back out into traffic toward the wing area, where other defenders can help. A successful baseline drive yields a very high-percentage offensive shot.

5. Avoid Bad Fouls. Most fouls are costly and should be avoided. They arise from sloppy play and are not necessary. Sure, there are times to foul: stopping an otherwise easy lay-up, trying to regain possession in the final minutes of the game, fouling a player who is a terrible foul shooter. Also, there *are* good fouls, particularly when the defense has not accumulated many fouls, and the player thinks he can take the ball away from a mediocre ballhandler. He reaches in and risks the referee's call.

However, when the defense has accumulated seven fouls, the other team shoots a one-and-one foul shot. At that point, usually late in the game, fouls can become very costly. Also, once a player personally accumulates five fouls, he is ejected from the game. The big players tend to accumulate the most fouls, since there is so much action underneath the hoop. Young kids tend to get sloppy and can accumulate fouls rapidly.

It's very easy to make body contact underneath. Any movement of the defensive player, when attempting to block a shot, will usually result in a foul call. Many youth referees will blow the whistle automatically on attempts to block a shot, if the players' bodies are close. When defending a short jump shot under the hoop, where bodies are always touching, the best recourse is for a player to just stand still and erect, hands straight up. (See figure 4-2 again.) I call this "stick 'em up!" It may result in two points for the opposing team, but this defensive stance puts at least some pressure on the shot. It can also draw an offensive foul. At the very least, it saves your big player from foul trouble.

6. Deny the Ball. A central defensive concept is to deny passes to your opponent, especially when she is in close to the hoop. A defensive player can deny a pass by obstructing the space between the ball and the player he is guarding, or otherwise guarding the passer so closely that he has doubts about passing. This is a cornerstone of defensive strategy. All teams must focus on it.

If a player, especially a big player, is in a low post close to the hoop, she will generally score if she gets the ball. The idea is to ensure she doesn't get it by fronting her, that is, playing between her and the ball. At the very least, the defensive player should play to her inside, snuggling up close with an arm in front of her and obstructing the passing lane.

Fronting generally works only close to the hoop, within five to six feet of it. When a defensive player is fronting a low-post player, he should get right in front, leaning into her. He should try subtly to push her farther underneath, with one hand very high to deny the high passing lane and the other hand in contact to "feel" the opponent.

7-4. DENY THE PASS

The passing lane underneath the hoop must be denied the offense by a player extending the arm into the lane, or, better, by fronting with the whole body.

Farther from the hoop, a defender should discourage a pass by using her extended hand, but should stay slightly behind the receiver to prevent an alley-oop pass over the head.

If fronting is attempted too far from the hoop, a passer can effectively break the defense by making an alley-oop pass over the fronting defender. So, if a player is out beyond the low-post area, he should not front her opponent. In this case, she should snuggle up very close, on the ball-side of the post player, with her back foot about twelve inches behind and a hand in the passing lane. A player should front only when an offensive player is flashing back and forth under the hoop or in a low post. Nonetheless, sometimes a defender will be caught fronting too far out from the hoop, and another defensive player must help out if the alley-oop succeeds. (See figure 7-4.) See defensive concept nine on page 126 for information on denying passes out on the perimeter.

Deny-Corner Drill. Line up two lines, one for offensive forwards by the corner and one for defensive forwards. The coach has the ball and tries to pass into the corner. The defender tries to deny the pass and, at the same time, watch for back-door moves. The offensive forward v-cuts to try to get free.

Deny-Wing Drill. This is the same as the deny-corner drill, except the guards line up in the wing area.

7. Fight Through or Around the Pick. I have discussed this already, but it bears repeating here: The best way to defend a pick is to fight through it. Usually, other defensive teammates will see the pick as it is being formed and alert the player being screened, so she can try to avoid the pick. They yell out, "Screen Left!" The defender can then take a quick look and see if there is room to step through the screen, that is, quickly squeeze between the screener and the ball carrier without fouling. If the ball carrier is dribbling to the right, the player should step up with the left foot to get a bit in front of the screen, push the stomach and hips out a bit, feel the screener with her left hand, then slide over the screen. Another option is for her to sink behind the screener, that is, step behind the screener and pick up the dribbler on the other side. The defender who was covering the screener should also step back to let her through, but be prepared to call a switch quickly if needed. Sinking back works better on the perimeter, well away from the hoop, but, if used too close to the hoop, it can enable an uncontested shot.

However, when an offensive screen or pick is successful, the defense must adjust and switch. The free defender, the one guarding the screener, must shout out "Switch!" This alerts the player being screened to now guard the screener. Switching is a tricky move but can be an effective defense to a pick or screen. The free defender must now cover the dribbler.

Nevertheless, when a switch occurs, it's often just what the offense wanted. The screener is momentarily left alone and can usually roll into the lane in preparation for

7-5. **DEFEND THE PICK**

To defend against the pick, the defender (in the dark t-shirt, left) tries to step through the pick as her teammate begins to "show" herself to the dribbler.

a pass. So the defender who switched needs to hedge the bet a bit by showing herself to the ballhandler while still keeping an eye on the player she left alone. She is just trying to buy some time, slow things down, force the dribbler wide. The defender who was screened must drop back very quickly to help out. Other defenders need to adjust and pick up on what may be a 2-on-1 situation. (See figure 7-5.)

Rip-the-Screen Drill. Four players pair up, two on offense and two on defense. The two players with the ball stand about twelve feet apart near the top of the key. They pass the ball back and forth a few times, without indicating to the defenders when or who will initiate a screen. Defenders shouldn't try to steal the passes. At some point, one offensive player, after passing the ball, runs to screen his teammate's defender. The defenders must choose to switch (option A), fight through (option B), or sink back (option C). At first, have your players practice each option, then let the players choose the right one for the play.

8. Resist the Fake. Many coaches teach their players to focus on the ballhandler's belly, since that's the toughest thing to fake. Everything else may move in any direction, but the belly is least involved with the fake and must go where the ball goes. It's just much easier to fake with the eyes, head, ball, and feet. I think the advice is generally good, conceptu-

125

ally. However, a player really needs to stay in touch with the whole offensive player. The ball is what they want to get a hand on, so I say your players need to keep an eye on it. Tell them to stay low and see the ball, see the whole scene. In fact, I like to see players "track" the ball with the hand closest to it. Wherever the ball is, that hand is as close to it as possible, following it around. Then, if there is a chance for a steal or a tip, the hand will have started from the closest position. So emphasize the need to sense the center of the ballhandler's action and to keep a hand close to the ball, moving with it.

9. Steal the Ball; Ball-You-Player. In youth basketball, many passes are stolen, and stealing the ball should always be on a player's mind. As noted, the defense must have the view that the ball is theirs and that the offense has no rights to it. Defense is a state of mind. I repeat this, and coaches need to do so as well. A younger player's passes are much softer and are often "telegraphed." A youngster who is looking to steal, who thinks about getting the ball, will pick up opportunities to steal just by observing the opponent's body and eye movements. However, many players don't even think about stealing the ball. They don't realize how easy it is. It's a state of mind.

Sometimes the passer will let the whole world know where the ball is going, making it easy to steal. The defender wants to position himself a bit to the ball side of the player he is guarding, that is, the side where the ballhandler is. This concept is called ball-you-player, the term "player" here referring to the player being guarded. This sig-

7–6. **BALL-YOU-PLAYER**

Player should cheat a bit toward the ball-side of opponent and, anticipating the pass, be in position to get a hand into the passing lane.

nifies that the defender should be between the ball and his opponent, that is, on the ball side of his opponent. If there is a pass, he is in position to steal. The hand closest to the ball is extended out, ready to block a pass. Tell your players to judge how far it is from their hand to the passing lane between two offensive players. Most kids don't realize that it's just a few feet, a distance they can travel in much less time than it takes the ball to get there. Tell them to picture an imaginary line between the ball and their opponent. The player does not have to catch the ball, it's only necessary to tip it away and then scoop it up. Body momentum will bring the player right to its bounce.

The steal move is simply a matter of sensing the right time to strike. The player waits until the passer, often a point guard or off guard, begins to turn to pass. Then they pick the right time and go. The defensive player should remember to thrust his ball-side hand into the passing lane. Obviously, if a player has exceptional quickness, if the passer is below average, or if the receiver fails to move toward the pass, then the defensive player should steal every time. Make sure he watches, though, because if the steal attempt fails, then the player is free, and a high-percentage shot is usually the result. Pass-stealing is like shooting. A player must be able to succeed most of the time or not try it. Players who are slower should continue to threaten passing lanes, but should focus more on defending their opponent than stealing. The best passes to steal are guard-to-wing or wing-to-corner. These passes usually occur during regular play patterns, so they can be anticipated better

7–7. **THE STEAL**

One of the prettiest plays in basketball is a well-timed steal, although few kids try this move.

than others. A player can cheat a bit, getting ready for the steal when he recognizes the play. At the very least, a good defensive position will be noticed by the passer and can effectively deny the passing lane, forcing the play elsewhere.

10. Boxing Out. Boxing out is a fundamental defensive move which must be made every time the ball is shot. It involves pivoting toward the player with the back side, elbows and legs spread, keeping oneself in between the offensive player and the hoop.

It's important in boxing out for the defensive player to make contact with his opponent and move with him. The contact will rarely be called a foul unless it is flagrant. Usually, the offensive player is also pushing; so it evens out, and no foul is called. Sometimes, a defender needs to hold the offensive player away from the hoop by maintaining contact; other times, it's sufficient for him to just momentarily bump him and move toward the hoop, particularly if they are more than five or six feet out. Your players should never get caught in too far under the hoop—little can be done in there because rebounds bounce out away from the basket. They should never let an opponent push them under the hoop, and they should always get a thigh or hip into the opponent to hold their ground.

Rebounding is a tough business. Most players love to mix it up, bumping and leaning on opponents underneath the basket. Rebounders need to be hungry, and it helps to be a bit ornery. Underneath is the world of grunts, groans, smacks, and ouches. Players, especially big players, need to understand that they must be intimidating and assert themselves within the limits of the rules. I'm not suggesting foul play, and a coach never should. In the long run, it will hurt a kid's psychological development. However, strong aggressive play is definitely needed underneath.

Boxer Drill. Station five players on the floor, two at low post, one at high post, one at wing and one at corner, defended by players of similar size. The coach passes freely to one player who shoots, the defenders box out, and all players try to rebound. Watch the players' form, the timing of the box out, and whether the defenders are keeping a hand in loose contact.

Rotate-'n'-Box Drill. Three players line up in a semi-circle twelve feet from the hoop; each has a defender midway between them. The coach shoots, calling left or right just before he shoots, signaling the defenders to rotate to the player in that direction, relative to them, and box out. (See figure 7-8.)

REBOUNDING

Rebounding is a skill required on both offense and defense, but the fact is that if defensive players are playing properly, they should ordinarily get two of three rebounds. Rebounding

128

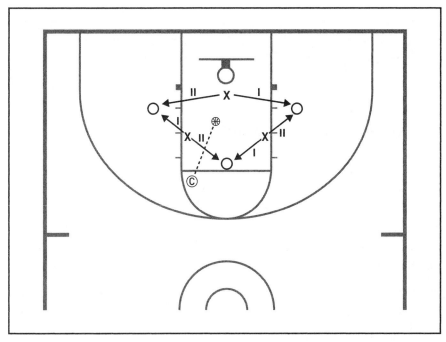

Defenders are midway between offensive players; as coach shoots and yells which way, they rotate and box opponent. Coach needs to shout so players have a chance, generally just before he releases.

has as much or more to do with floor position, technique, and strength than with height. This is why Bill Russell could routinely clean Wilt Chamberlain's clock underneath. Since the defender is usually between the man defended and the hoop, he is in an excellent position to box out or screen opponents from the ball. Defensive rebounding relies mainly on positioning and strength, while offensive rebounding also requires agility and movement. Defensive rebounding also requires more of a team effort, with everyone boxing out, while offensive rebounding is mainly an individual effort.

Floor position is the most important factor in rebounding, and judging where the ball will rebound is the key. There is plenty of time to get into position for rebounding. Usually the ball will bound off the hoop and continue to the opposite side from where it was shot. If shot along the baseline, it will bound to the opposite baseline; if shot from the wing, it will bound more sharply. If shot from a distance, it will usually bounce further out than if shot from up close. There is a period, called dead time or hang time, which is the time from when the ball leaves the shooter's hand until it gets to a position where it can be rebounded. This normally takes two seconds. A player's ability to be a good rebounder depends on how he uses this hang time. Instead of just watching the flight of the ball, he needs to get busy and anticipate where the ball will bounce, then head or step that way. He needs to see where his opponent is moving and set his box, if on defense, or make a move to get around the box if on offense, moving to the area where the ball is most likely to rebound and establish position.

OFFENSIVE REBOUNDING MOVES

Three good moves for players to think about in getting offensive rebounds are the fake; the arm over, step over; and the spin move. Often, a defender will look to see which way the offensive player is moving before he turns to box out, so the player on offense should fake one way and go the other. This makes it tougher to box out. The "arm-over, step-over" move can be used when a player is boxed out; he should raise his arm over the opponent's arm, and his leg over the opponent's leg, then step over the box. To do a spin move, the player fakes one way and then spins backwards around the opponent.

The Rebounding Jump. The rebounder jumps up, preferably straight up to avoid a foul. The rebounder should not go over another player who has better position—it's an easy foul for the referee to see.

Catching the Rebound. Caution players against getting into the habit of always tapping the rebound away. A well-placed tap against a bigger player may be needed, but players should always try to catch the ball forcefully with both hands and land well, both feet spread out. After catching the rebound, a player must then keep the ball high for an overhead outlet pass. If she must bring it down, she should do so with strength—elbows out, ball up just below the chin, legs wide—and pivot quickly. A lot of hands will attack the ball, so she needs to be ready and be quick. Players must be ready to fight for the ball. Often two players will grab a rebound at the same time, and the one who wants it the most, the one who fights for it, will get it most of the time.

As noted, nearly 75 percent of missed shots will rebound to the opposite side of the hoop, usually at an angle similar to or slightly greater than the shot angle. So, if a player has freedom and time to move, especially if no teammate is at the opposite side, he should head or lean that way.

Grab-It-Strong Drill. Have two players of similar size stand back to back, a foot or so apart. Throw a ball up about ten-feet high between them and let them turn and catch the "rebound." Foster aggressive play, but make sure they don't get carried away. Have a whistle ready.

130

Hit the Outlet. The first step after a defensive rebound is to pass to the outlet. Another player will have the responsibility to be there, so the rebounder should turn and fire. If he does it quickly, the pass will be open. He should not let the other players have time to regroup.

Rebounding Drill. Three to four shooters and three to four rebounders stand in a semicircle ten to fifteen feet from the hoop. Use shorter distance for younger players and forwards or centers. The coach takes a fifteen-foot shot that all players try to rebound. Each defensive player must box out her opponent, who tries to get around the box and get the rebound. Another good drill is for two players to practice rebounding by bouncing a ball off a wall, but make sure they don't collide with the wall.

Guess-the-Bounce Drill This great drill involves a player underneath and a shooting guard. The rebounder tries to position himself exactly where he thinks the ball will come. He must get there before it hits the basket. See how often he can get it right. The guard should shoot from different spots. It's good shooting practice, too!

FULL-COURT PRESS

Very young teams do not normally press. It's usually not allowed because kids have enough trouble dribbling or passing as it is. If they were allowed to press at very young ages, the ball would rarely get upcourt. By seventh or eighth grade, pressing is usually allowed. This is essentially a man-to-man and double-teaming defense for the entire length of the court, right from the inbound pass. Usually, one defender tries to pressure the inbound passer, and another stays between the other offensive guard and the ball. This forces a long, high inbound pass which is susceptible to interception. Just remember that someone has to stay back on defense, and others must get up the court quickly in case the press fails. Figure 7-9 on page 132 gives a good plan for the press. If the ball is inbounded with a short pass, both defenders quickly double-team. If a dribbler gets the pass and heads up the court along the sideline, the defender cuts him off, slowing him down and allowing for another double-team opportunity.

ZONE DEFENSE

Most coaches tend to agree that the rules of amateur basketball should be changed to limit zone defenses or prohibit it, as the pros do. A growing number of youth leagues do prohibit this kind of defense. Zone defense is the lazy player's defense

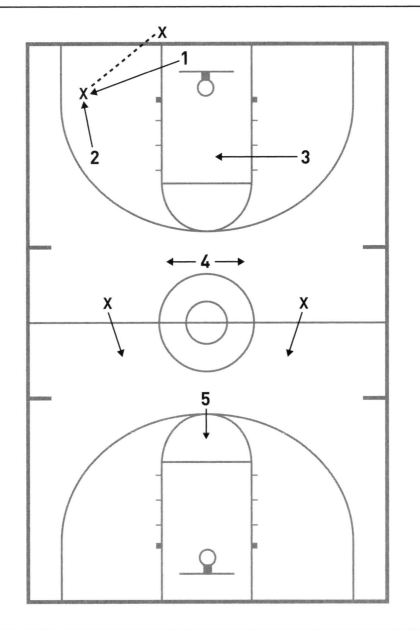

and requires much less skill. In a zone, every defender stays near the lane area, low and high post, preventing the inside play. Thus, the offense must shoot from outside, and the kids don't really learn defense; they just clog up the lanes. It's not what the game was meant to be. When adult players play pick-up games, they usually use a man-to-man defense.

On the other hand, a zone is a much easier defense for kids to learn. Moreover, since kids don't shoot long shots very well, and since the zone works best to stop scoring in close to the basket, zone defense works well at youth levels. Therefore, you will see coaches use it, and you will need to consider using it to remain competitive.

TEACHING ZONE DEFENSE

Zone defenses are easy to teach, and they are effective, particularly against a good team or a team that does not have good outside shooting. Also, the vast skill differences and size differences in third through seventh grade make a zone suitable, since the zone defense does not allow one player to dominate the game. The zone defenses are usually a 1-2-2, a 2-1-2, a 1-3-1, or a 2-3. (See figure 7-10 on page 134.)

The entire zone formation should shift to the left or to the right, depending on where the ball is. Defensive players front any opponents underneath, to deny the inside pass and force the offense to shoot from outside. If the ball is passed into the corner, an opportunity to trap that player arises, and the baseline and wing defender should do so if they are available.

The weakest parts of the zone are the seams, the areas in between the defenders. Zone defenders are concentrating primarily on their individual areas and not just on one opponent, so a quick pass and shot from a seam can catch a defender off guard. This is especially true in a 2-3, where the foul line area is usually open. The 1-3-1 stops the center jump shot and allows for good trapping, but its corners and baselines are exposed. The 1-2-2 zone defense exposes the lane to penetration up the middle. The 2-1-2 seems to be most popular at grade-school-level play. A more advanced

◀ The defense lines up as shown here. #1 aggressively closes the middle, forcing the ball to be inbounded into the corner. Depending upon which side of the court the ball is inbounded from, #1 and #2 (or #3) trap the dribbler. #1 also tries to position himself to close down a passing lane. If the ball is passed back to the inbounder, players trap him. The player (#2 or #3) not involved in the trap drops back into a passing lane to intercept the pass. #4 roves along the mid-court, also looking to intercept a pass. #5 defends the hoop and must not let a pass get over his head.

7–10. **ZONE DEFENSES**

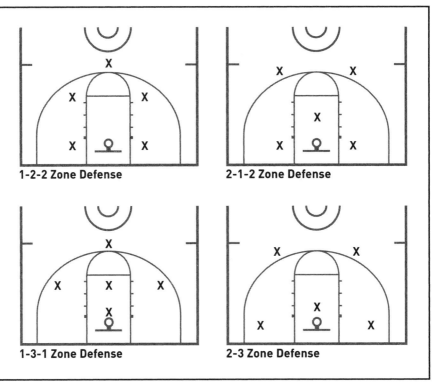

1-2-2 Zone Defense

2-1-2 Zone Defense

1-3-1 Zone Defense

2-3 Zone Defense

Zone defenses are easy to teach and are especially effective in younger-aged teams where abilities and sizes can vary greatly. Some typical zone defenses are show here.

zone is the box and chaser, which defends the four post positions and provides a free defender to pressure the ball.

MAN-TO-MAN DEFENSE

A man-to-man defense allows for a more open and exciting game. Players are pitted against each other, one-on-one, and the skill level is more challenging. In man-to-man defense, a player guards her position's counterpart, usually matching up with a player of equal height and skill. She stays between that player and the basket at all times, whether that player has the ball or not. Kids learn more in this kind of defense, and they know they are responsible for stopping their opponent. It's real defense. It requires better conditioning and better skills and makes a more interesting game to play and to watch. That's why the pros do it that way.

DEFENSIVE DRILLS

The Slip-Slide Drill. Four players line up across one end of the court and slide-step sideways to the other end. The drill requires each player to take three steps toward one side and then three to the other, moving backward all the time. Coaches must ensure that players' bodies are kept low with arms out and up, that their legs don't cross, and that they take short, quick steps.

No-Arm-Shuffle Drill. Two dribblers and two defenders start at one end of the court. Each pair should use only one-half of the court's width. The defender may not use his hands, but clasps them in front. She must endeavor to stay in front of the ball and pressure the dribbler as he moves down the court. She should stay low, not cross her legs, and take quick, short strides. The dribbler tries to lose the defender and shoot a lay-up. If the dribbler passes the defender, the defender must turn and catch up.

Vertical-Leap Drill. Players should all have a spot on a wall which represents their highest leap to date and should try to better the mark each day. Often a funny dimple in a concrete wall is enough for a marker. Players should also measure the distance between their highest reach flat-footed and their highest point jumping. Record these statistics.

Positioning Drill. Two players assume offensive and defensive stances out in the wing area. The coach stands in the key with the ball. The offensive player tries to maneuver free for a pass. The defender tries to deny him. The coach passes only if the offensive player gets a step on the defender.

07

08 RUNNING A PRACTICE

Perhaps the most common questions I get from beginner coaches and parents in any sport are, "How do I start?" and "How do I run a practice?" The short answer is to have players pass, dribble, and shoot basketballs until their arms fall off. The long answer follows.

GETTING STARTED

The job starts on day one! A month or so before the first practice, you should communicate with your team and the parents on a number of matters. You should suggest to parents that their child will have a much easier start if he or she shows up in decent shape. Basketball doesn't require the strength of some other sports, but it does require endurance, quickness, and agility. It's best, particularly at grade-school levels, if players are able to do a half dozen thirty-yard wind sprints without requiring an ambulance. They should also to be able to do pushups, at least five at younger ages, ten at intermediate. Younger kids won't have the upper body strength, but get them started. They should do what they can, and then strive for just one more! This means they should work at least every other day for a few weeks to get up to this level.

Players and parents also need to know that practices are important and that being on time is important for them and for the team. The game schedule, practice schedule, and starting and ending times should all be communicated when the information is available so parents can begin arranging for transportation, etc.

You should also communicate that you welcome help. At least two assistant coaches are needed; three are better. A team "parent" or two is needed to help with incidentals like uniforms, candy drives, and organizing car pools. Ask for help! A sample letter to parents follows.

136

Dear Parent/Guardian,

Welcome to the (Name) Basketball program. Our season starts in three weeks, and I'd like to go over a few things that will help us get off to a great start!

Practices will start on (Date), and we will have practice every Tuesday thereafter. We'll practice for one hour from 6:30 to 7:30 p.m. It's important that your child arrive on time (a few minutes early is fine) and be picked up on time. Sneakers are required at practices and games. Players can bring water, although a water fountain is available. Our games will be on Saturday mornings, and the starting time may vary a bit; we'll get a detailed schedule out as soon as possible. Please send me your e-mail address to facilitate quick communication. My e-mail is jackmc@hoopsrgreat.go.

It would be very helpful to your child to do some mild conditioning before the season starts, so that initial practices are not too tiring. Jogging, wind sprints (six for thirty yards), and pushups (build up to at least five to ten) are fine. I also suggest they do some dribbling. It can be done on any hard surface, even in the cellar, and you don't need a basket! Dribbling is a most important skill at young ages, and it will give your child an edge to start early.

I promote parental involvement. I need a few assistant coaches. Don't worry about experience; we can all learn as we go. There is a great book out called *COACHING YOUTH BASKETBALL: The Guide for Coaches, Parents and Athletes*, by John P. McCarthy, and I recommend you obtain it. I also need a team parent or two to help organize things. If you are interested, give me a call or see me at the first practice.

My philosophy is to help your child learn the skills and fundamentals of, become better at, and have fun with the great game of basketball. Most kids do not go on to play at advanced levels, but if they learn the basics, they will enjoy the game for their whole lives. Every child will play in every game (state the league rule about minimum playing time). Those who work harder may get some additional playing time, but they must earn it! Winning is fun, but it is not important, and not at all as important as making this a positive learning experience. (If your league does not even keep score, at this age, say so).

I hope you will keep this in mind when rooting for the team or your child at games. It's helpful to praise good hustle or effort, but it is not helpful to

08

give specific instructions to your child during play (that's my role) or to comment on referee calls (they are learning, too). I will not allow criticism from parents or other players.

It is most helpful for a parent to work with their child at home to improve skills. Having a catch, practicing rebounding for shots, and encouraging dribbling will lead to rapid improvement. Practice definitely leads to improvement, and so more is always better! A little one-on-one will also help (and give you some exercise, too). Encourage kids to get together for small games, two-on-two, or three-on-three.

Of course, if your schedule does not permit the above, you have already taken a big step by allowing your child to be involved and by providing transportation. Welcome aboard!

Best Regards,
Coach Jack McCarthy
Phone #, e-mail, address

REINFORCE THE BASICS

The other thing kids need to do early is learn the basics of the game. Kids learn to understand basketball at a pretty young age, but you shouldn't assume too much. Most importantly, tell parents about this book! Tell them to read it. It's written for parents as much as for coaches, and they can be a great help to you if they get involved early on in explaining the game and instructing their children. As noted above, remind parents that they should encourage their children to spend some time each day dribbling the ball on any hard surface. If there is a hoop around, then add in some practice with lay-ups, foul shots, and jumpers. Dribbling and lay-ups are most important for beginners.

FIND EXTRA PRACTICE TIME

Unfortunately, you will probably not get as much practice time for your team as you want or need. Clinics for beginners play once or twice a week. Club teams may practice twice during the week and play on weekends. School teams may practice more regularly. Access to gyms is sought by all kinds of programs during winter in northern states, and so they often must be shared by many. An enterprising coach can find a way to get more practice, but it's not the rule. Clearly the best practice condition is on a regulation court, but any hard surface will do for dribbling and passing, as well as for conditioning. A trip to the local YMCA is an excellent alternative. Videotape scrimmages, and plan an evening at someone's house to view them, maybe with some pizza. There are many ways to gain additional practice, even if it's only to urge mom and dad, or big brother or sister, to spend thirty minutes rebounding shots or mildly pressuring a player while dribbling. Advise parents as to shortcomings in their child's form so they can help make needed changes. The more you get your players drilling their skills, the better your team will be! That's the surest thing about any sport. A coach must find creative ways to get players more practice time. Sure, you may not be able to spend every night on it, but that's where parents and assistant coaches come in.

IDENTIFY YOUR GOALS

There are five key objectives you need to consider for each practice plan. Their relative importance will vary a bit as you get further into the season, and they also vary depending upon what age group you work with, but these concepts are always important and should be part of your plan for each practice.

FIVE KEY GOALS FOR PRACTICES
1. Get the players in shape.
2. Understand each player's potential.
3. Work on individual skills and position skills.
4. Work on making them a team with sharp execution of plays and defenses.
5. Motivate, Communicate, Lead.

Basketball practices typically last for one to two hours at grade-school levels, depending on the day of the week and on gym availability. Grade-school teams, which practice a few days a week (or more), often go for an hour and a half after school. Beginner teams in clinic programs often only get an hour of gym time for practice. All five goals listed above should be considered each time you prepare a practice plan (we'll get to what a practice plan looks like a bit later). In a two-hour practice, I would devote ten minutes to chatter and water breaks, fifteen to twenty minutes to conditioning, thirty minutes to shooting and offensive drills, thirty minutes to defensive skills, thirty minutes to team dynamics, and thirty minutes to scrimmages. Doesn't add up to two hours, does it? It will if you can do a few things at the same time! See my presentation on the Stations concept below. In fact, if you have many parent-coaches helping out, you can nearly double each of these time frames. The worst thing in a practice is to have kids standing around a lot, watching. They need time with the ball!

Early in the season, you should spend time on conditioning, speed, and agility drills, and most of the time on fundamental skills such as dribbling, passing, and shooting. After a while, add in play patterns. Later in the season, you need to spend more time on specialty drills and refinements.

Let's discuss each goal.

FIRST GOAL: GET THE PLAYERS IN SHAPE

Conditioning is more important in basketball than any other major sport. Frankly, it doesn't take much to get grade-school or high-school kids into shape, and there is just no excuse when they aren't. If you want to give your team an edge, get them in great shape: A lot of games are won when the other team is tired. Basketball requires endurance. Improvement can come from some strength training and speed and agility drills. The worst mistake is to assume that the kids will get themselves into shape. Coaches tend to underestimate the value of conditioning, but kids in shape win close games. Even if you only get your kids to double the number of pushups they can do and run some sprints regularly, they will be better players. At the very least, you need to warm up and stretch muscles before practice. *Warm-ups should never be passed over.*

There are a few do's and don'ts about getting players in shape.

Do: Warm Up

Make sure players warm up before practice. Early in the season, the large muscles high on the inner thigh and groin area and the shins are vulnerable. If the kids come in from outside, ankles and knees are cold. Most ballplayers have experienced muscular or joint strains or sprains or suffered from shin splints; these injuries can take weeks to heal. Tell your players that muscles are like bubble gum. Unless they stretch slowly, they will tear. Lay-ups are great warm-ups. A few laps around the gym at a slow pace should get your players to break a sweat and warm up major leg muscles. Tell them to run backward and shuffle-step part of the time.

Warm-ups can start before your practice starting time, so tell players to arrive a few minutes early. Don't expect players to warm up sufficiently on their own. They should be told to stretch out on their own before practice, but you should warm up the team together. Players who aren't warmed-up get hurt too easily. (See figure 8-1 for good stretches.)

8-1. **BEST FOUR STRETCHES**

The Hurdler is a good method for stretching the legs. A player sits on the ground with one leg forward and the other bent inward. She touches the big toe of the extended foot for five to ten seconds.

A good thigh stretch technique is for the player to stand with the legs spread sideways, then lean to one side, bending the knee. This stretches the opposite thigh muscle.

To stretch the quadricep while standing, player stands on one leg while pulling the other leg up behind the buttocks.

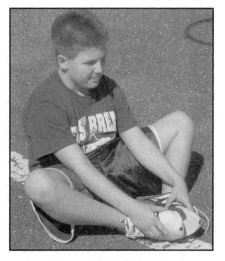

The Butterfly, a great stretch for large groin muscles and tendons. Player sits and places soles of sneakers together. Pulls toes in and knees down.

Quick Cali Set. Start the team off with what I call the Quick Cali Set: twenty-five jumping jacks, ten to twenty pushups, fifteen half-sit-ups, a dozen toe touches with legs crossed, and twenty trunk turns.

Leg Stretches. (See figure 8-1.) Do a few from the Leg Stretch Set. Leg stretches should be done smoothly without jerking or straining. A few good ones are:

1. **Toe-hand**: The player lies on his back with arms stretched outward, on the floor. He alternately brings each foot up and over to the opposite hand.
2. **Hurdler:** The player sits on the ground with one leg forward and one bent inward. He touches and holds the forward toe for five seconds. He reverses legs and repeats.
3. **Standing Quadriceps:** Standing on one leg, the player lifts the other foot from behind to touch the buttocks.
4. **Supine Hamstring**: Lying on the back with hands behind one knee, the player pulls that leg, as straight-legged as possible, toward the chest. He repeats with the other leg. No jerking movements, and no bobbing up and down!
5. **Thigh Stretch**: Standing with legs outstretched sideways, the player leans to one side, bending that knee, to stretch the opposite thigh muscle.
6. **Achilles and Calf Stretch**: The player places one foot a step in front of the other. He leans forward and bends the front leg, stretching the lower part of the back leg. He switches legs and repeats.
7. **Butterfly Groin:** One of the best stretches is for the player to sit on the ground and place the soles of his sneakers together. Then he gently pulls his feet in close for fifteen seconds, relaxes, then pulls in again. He repeats three to four times.

Jumping. Players should also do some jumping warm-ups. A good one is for the player to hop a few times on one foot, squat on both feet and touch the floor, hop a few times on the other foot, squat again, then burst up in a two-legged, full high jump. Jumping rope is also an excellent warm-up and improves jumping ability and agility.

After all of this, players should pair up and shoot free throws or work on an individual skill you have advised them to improve upon until you are ready to start practice. For leaping conditioning, see the next chapter's discussion on plyometrics.

Do: Start on Time!

Latecomers must catch up and do additional pushups (if they can't do regular pushups, then have them do them off the knees). The team captain or an assistant can lead the warm-up exercises while you get organized, check to see who is there, and talk to coaches or parents.

Do: Monitor Your Players

Don't overwork players! Some coaches have their kids running all the time, all season long. The players are young, but there are limits even for the young. By the same token, there might be periods when players are just standing around. Here are some exercises players can do when they have free time during a practice.

Strength Enhancers. I believe that pushups are the best single exercise for building upper-body strength in kids (along with sit-ups). Hand out sets of twenty pushups or sit-ups freely. Another great strength enhancer is what I call the wrist machine. It's simply a two-foot section of broom handle or thick pipe, with four feet of clothesline attached to the center and a five-to-ten-pound weight attached to the other end of the line. The player holds the bar with arms outstretched, and coils or rolls the bar and the line around it until the weight rises to reach the bar. He lowers the line and does the exercise twice more. It's great for wrists and forearms and leads to the ability to pass crisply. I have kids work on it when not engaged in a scrimmage. Have one lying around, handy. Stress to your players that these exercises will give them an edge they will need when they come up against their opponents. If a kid does fifty pushups a day, he will become very strong! Judge what a player can do, and slightly push his limit. Don't ask him to do something that will embarrass him, however.

Don't: Encourage Formal Weight Training

I generally recommend avoiding formal weight training for grade-school kids since they are still growing at a rapid pace. However, there is a different view, and I'll present it in chapter ten, on formal conditioning.

Don't: Do Wind Sprints at the Beginning of Practice

Wind sprints require the loosest muscles, so they should normally be done at the end of practice. Even then keep them short: ten to twenty yards at first, working up to thirty.

The suicide drill is a great sprint drill for ending practice. The kids start at the end line, sprint to the top of the key, touch the floor, and sprint back to the end line and touch the floor. They sprint to half-court and back in the same manner. They finish up with the backcourt key and finally a full-court sprint. The whole exercise involves eight sprints. Time them. Tell the players to reach out in a long stride. Have them do some backward and some sideways.

Finish practice with a few half-court races. Wind sprints are essential for endurance and leg strength. If they are waiting for their parents, remind them that foul shots are hardest to shoot when very tired, and the best time to get a few in is after sprints.

Speed and Leaping Improvement Drills

You can't do much to make a slow kid a lot faster; but you can improve speed somewhat, and you can improve running strength, agility, and balance by a good deal.

Some good drills to improve running speed and form are:

The Robot Drill. Line up the players and have them run full-court at half-speed, alternatively driving their fists downward from neck-height to just behind the buttocks with each stride. The idea is for the players to bang or drive their fists downward in a robotic cadence in rhythm with their stride. The arms are bent to start but can be straightened into whatever position is comfortable. Look at track stars in the 100-yard dash, and observe how they pump the arms. Have players run this drill three times, increasing speed each time.

The Bounce. This is similar to the robot, except players concentrate on lifting their knees as high as possible toward the chest, bouncing off the ground with each step. This drill, routinely done by sprinters and high jumpers, develops the power thrust needed to sprint. Try to incorporate the robot drill with this one after a while.

The Buttkick Drill. The players again run forty yards and return, this time kicking their heels into their buttocks. This helps the follow-through needed for a complete stride. Players need every bit of thrust to sprint.

The Goose-Step Drill. Finally, have players run forty yards in a goose step, kicking their legs straight out and lifting them vertically and high. This drill develops a greater stride.

Agility Drills

Simon-Says Drill. Line up players in five lines. Have the first row of five start running in place, body low, taking short, quick, choppy steps. Using your hand, signal the players to shuffle laterally (without crossing the feet), forward, backward, and downward to the ground. Players must square the shoulders, stay low, and react quickly. Have them go for twenty seconds, then repeat the drill with a new row of players.

Carioca Drill. Players line up as for the simon-says drill, then carioca, that is, run sideways, left foot over right, then left foot behind right, for forty yards. Have them repeat four times.

144

SECOND GOAL: UNDERSTAND EACH PLAYER'S POTENTIAL

You need to figure out what each player can do, so he can concentrate on developing the specific skills needed in his position.

Generally, bigger kids play underneath and smaller kids are guards, but not necessarily. Some big kids have remarkable ballhandling and passing skills, and these should be developed. Some average-sized kids have great leaping ability and have a knack at getting into position for rebounds. So keep an open mind and figure out what players you need to move around a bit. I've seen many coaches decide too quickly who plays where and then never change it. I have also seen a coach stick someone in an odd position, late in a meaningless game, and suddenly find that the kid was a natural there. While it's important to get things set early in order to concentrate on the special skills required by each position, you should always be looking to see if a player could help the team somewhere else. Assistant coaches can help you a lot here. Some kids are lousy at practice and come alive in a game; some are the opposite and can't play under pressure.

Keep Track of Players' Strengths

A good way to do this is to start making lists. Run sprints to see who your fastest players are. Who can accelerate the best, that is, has the best short-distance time? Who are the most agile? Who are the risk-takers, the fiercest defenders, the strongest players? Who has the best hands? Who wants the ball the most? Who are the natural leaders? Who has a three-point shot, a jumper, a great foul-shot percentage? Who can dribble, pass, follow play patterns to the letter? Who made a clutch play?

Once you create these lists, don't throw them away. Check them every couple of weeks, and see if someone has earned another look. The lists are helpful since they force you to evaluate your players according to different aspects of athletic ability. Sometimes you will be surprised to see a name pop up for a player you hadn't been looking at very closely.

Constantly evaluate and reevaluate your players. It's incredible to me how rarely some coaches will discuss each player. It is simply far too easy to oversee a quiet kid who may have good ability. Perhaps an assistant coach has seen something that can surface in a full review. Don't just label someone for the season. Reconsider constantly. Give a kid a shot at something else if he is not working out where you first placed him.

Talk With Your Players

You will find many brief opportunities on the gym floor to talk to your players. How is school? Is anything troubling you? How are things at home? What are your interests? You

145

can find out a lot about a kid in a few minutes to help you understand the player, and you will also begin to earn her respect. Kids who like and respect you are more coachable.

THIRD GOAL: WORK ON INDIVIDUAL SKILLS

After fifteen to twenty minutes in a ninety-minute practice (less in mid-season) of conditioning, stretching, and speed and agility drills, I like to call the players together and give them an overview of what they will be doing in practice and what we expect of them. You might post the practice plan, so they know what's coming. Details can be supplied later.

The drills for individual development are generally found in chapters two through five. I won't repeat them, but will list them again in the sample practice plan later in this chapter.

Videotape Practices

Focus practice at first on individual form, skills, and fundamentals. I think it's a great idea to film kids at practice, especially scrimmages. Try to get a parent to volunteer to take some shots of players working on form and shooting, as well as running drills. Welcome parents to video their own child. Circulate the tapes to kids who need to see what they are doing wrong. You can all meet at someone's house to view the films and talk about form. In coaching, as in art, a picture is truly worth a thousand words.

Working on form and fundamentals early in the season on a regular basis is essential, and videotapes will help you here. Good form will go a long way; rely upon it! Kids shoot from the chest until sixth or seventh grade, and it's a very tough transition to a one-hand jump shot from a nice cradle. If a shooter leans back too far or has poor wrist and hand form, if a guard is not passing to open space, if a low triple-threat posture is not being used, or if forwards don't box out, let them know. There is no excuse for poor form. A player may not be able to hit every shot or execute every play pattern well, but he can always employ proper form, and form alone will help! Have the checklist at the end of the book handy to check a player's form.

Putting Drills Into Practice

It is helpful at times to divide the team into two groups for skills drills, with guards in one and forwards and centers in another, on either end of the court. I start with defensive drills, then do offensive drills. Then we just shoot for a while or do team drills. Kids love this part of the practice. It's better to have them shooting when they are a bit tired already.

Let the kids know they're doing the drills so that their skills become automatic and will be there for them under pressure. Let them know the objective of each drill, what

146

skill you are looking to improve. I believe it's better to keep drills short and fast-paced. Several repetitions for each player are enough. Better to use multiple drills than wear one out. By mid-season you want to compact conditioning and skill drills, so they take less time. Later in this chapter, I'll provide a plan for "stations" to help with this.

FOURTH GOAL: TEAMWORK PRACTICE

The last half-hour or so of practice is a good time to get the whole team together for drills that require two full teams on the floor. For teamwork drills, players should generally be assigned to their regular positions, once those positions have been established. The drills covering team play and play patterns, listed in the practice plan later in this chapter, are generally found in chapters six and seven.

Early in the pre-season, particularly for beginners, you can table this part of practice, since you need to focus on fundamentals and conditioning above all. Gradually, you will work up to about an hour (in a two-hour practice) during mid-season practices for teamwork, including a scrimmage.

Scrimmages are fun for the kids, and even fifteen minutes at the end of practice is a good idea. However, in the first weeks of pre-season they have much to learn, and there will be little time for anything else.

FIFTH GOAL: MOTIVATE, COMMUNICATE, LEAD, AND MAKE IT FUN

I devote much of chapter nine to this topic, but I'll preview the concept here. Many coaches seem to spend a lot of time hollering, trying to motivate players and get them to increase their concentration.

Frankly, whereas high energy is sometimes useful and you may occasionally have to yell to be heard, the screamer routine is often quite overdone. Furthermore, there is a line that shouldn't be crossed, and that line is when your tone humiliates a player. The idea is to be firm, to let players know that they can do better if they focus a bit more.

Ask yourself what your ultimate goal is. To win? To help a young boy or girl learn how to face challenges? If the latter is at least a significant part of your reason for coaching (as it should be), then try the positive reinforcement methods described in chapter nine. Stress that the player needs to be more productive to get more playing time. Coach a kid according to his needs. Some need caring; some need a gentle boot in the can; some need patience.

Most importantly, reward good effort. Praise good hustle. Yell out, "That's basketball!" It can get infectious. You are the leader of the team, the most significant person out there. What do you want their memory of you to be?

147

At young ages, you need to make practice fun. Many of the drills are little games themselves, so use them to keep interest up. Positive energy, however, is the key.

RUNNING A PRACTICE

SETTING UP STATIONS

One final word about specialty drills and parents. I once had six parents, men and women, on the court helping out. I had twelve kids on the team. I set up what we call stations, a group of simultaneous drills on separate areas of the court. Each parent ran one of the six rotations involving two kids each.

The drills in each station are competitive, so keep scores to see who does the best. Each drill lasts for five or so minutes, then the kids rotate to the next station until they have each performed all six stations. A parent or coach stays with each station and becomes knowledgeable about the skill being worked on there. Chapters three, four, and five each list a dozen or more drills for shooting, dribbling, and passing. Pick one or two drills from *each* skill and set up three to six stations. Tell assistant coaches what to do and look for. It's better if you are free to walk around and give instructions rather than be tied in to one station. If you only have three coaches/parents, then do one drill for each skill. The stations practice will yield a maximum of ball-touching in a minimum of time, and time is precious! Here are more drills.

Skills Stations

Shooting. Choose one or two drills depending on how many stations you can monitor. The best ones are lay-ups, short jump shots (coach rebounds), medley drill, and foul shots. One-on-one is another good drill.

Dribbling. There are many dribbling drills. I favored cone dribbling, sprint drill, fake-and-shake, and keep-away. Try different ones. Adjust the difficulty as you go.

Passing. Good passing drills are two quick, on the run, monkey in the middle, and give and go.

That's it. I rotate the players from station to station, using thirty minutes for the whole deal. The kids get the equivalent experience of six single-coach practices. You can make the exercise longer or shorter and design your own stations. If there is a scrimmage going on, find a spot for the subs to do some drills while waiting.

Position Stations

As noted earlier, I don't like to lock a kid into a position too early, so general skills drills are sufficient for beginners. At intermediate levels, I'd set up stations specifically for post players, perimeter players, and point guards to develop and fine-tune individual position skills. Players don't rotate, but do one or two drills at each station. Start with these and vary as needed.

Post Players. Drills include post-it drill, boxer drill, medley-shooting drill, rebounding drill.

Perimeter Players, Shooting Guards and Forwards. Drills are two-step drill, corner- and wing-shots drill, baseline drives, rotate-'n'-box drill.

Point Guard. Do sprint drill, floor-visioning drill, zigzag drill.

THE PRACTICE PLAN

Each practice should follow a written practice plan. It just takes a few minutes to think through what you want to accomplish, and it does wonders for efficient use of time. A practice plan follows a general routine. It varies somewhat in the proportion of time spent on areas as the season moves along and the actual drills used (mix them up for variety).

During the first weeks in the season, your plan should focus on (1) conditioning, (2) individual skills development, (3) evaluating your players, and (4) "homework" time spent looking at play patterns. Note that I said focus—all of these concepts are involved in every practice all year.

THE PLAN FOR BEGINNERS

At the clinic or recreation level, you will often have only an hour, once a week, for practice. It's simply not enough time, and you should try to find opportunities to do more. The best players are found out on a court on most nice days, but at least one additional session every week or so is very helpful. You don't want to go overboard or push too hard, but urge parents to provide opportunities for an eager young player to play. If the weather is warm enough, find an outside court you can get some time on. Practice is the key to improving skills. Tell the kids and parents to work on their own, especially on dribbling and lay-ups. At younger ages, you can shorten the conditioning a bit, but make sure you do at least ten minutes and spend some time talking basket-ball. Get them in a circle and ask them questions: "What's a foul?" "What's a walk or a double-dribble?" "Who can name the floor positions?" "What's a lay-up?" "A jump

149

shot?" "A hook or a three-pointer?" "What is meant by 'three seconds'?" "What are the various names for things around the court?"

Gather all the players around the key and demonstrate proper stance, particularly shooting from triple-threat, screening, and boxing out. Tell them about bad form. Look at specific parts of their body, hands, and footwork, to pick up on form issues. Demonstrate defensive form. When coaching beginners, it's important to spend a fair amount of time on this each practice, until they start to get a feel for the jargon and the rules of basketball. Use the glossary in the back of this book. After a while, you'll know when they get it.

With kids at young ages, it will take longer to teach drills, but make sure you acquaint the players with every concept and walk through drills. Have your coaches or parents read sections of the book so they can help during drills.

Daily Practice Schedule

1. **Conditioning.** Ten minutes. Quick cali set, a few from the leg-stretch set, such as butterfly and hurdler drills. Occasionally insert a speed drill: robot, bounce, butt-kick, goosestep. Include an agility drill: simon-says or carioca or a jumping drill.

2. **Skills Stations.** Twenty minutes. Set up three to six stations, with two drills each on dribbling, passing, and rebounding. Rotate about every four to six minutes. It will take longer at first to set up the stations, but after a few practices, these drills can move very quickly. Occasionally devote the skills period to position or shooting stations, as described above, with drills such as 21-jumper, 21-lay-up and 50-freebies. Have players shoot from their optimum location. Each player needs to find and know their range, then slowly extend it. Remind them they generally need to practice shots on their own, but you need to observe form every so often.

3. **Slow Scrimmage.** Twenty minutes. Set kids up in a half-court offense against five defenders. At first, defense can't use their hands. Have the offense pass to wing and then underneath, or drive and shoot. Coach them on the run, but stop play to make an important point. The idea is to get them used to passing, dribbling, pivoting, and shooting under light pressure. Keep the same team on offense for several tries, then switch. After a few practices, let them rotate with the rebound. After some time, allow the defense to use their hands. Tell kids to screen for someone and always look for opportunities to screen. Have post players flash back and forth and screen for each other. At some point, introduce the scissor, outside give and go, and post interchange plays (one at a time).

4. **Full Scrimmage.** Ten minutes. It won't be pretty at first, but you've got to start somewhere. Call out violations, but try not to stop play.

INTERMEDIATE AND ADVANCED PRACTICES

The following are typical sample-practice plans for different weeks during a season. The major segments of each plan are usually the same. First you do conditioning, then defensive skills practice, offensive skills practice, shooting practice, and team dynamics. Finish with sprints and closing comments. Most non-school teams start practice in the evenings during the weekdays, since coaches at grade-school levels have day jobs. Some of you will be able to start right after school. The practice plan I include below is for two hours. If you have two and a half hours, then expand sessions according to what's needed at a given point in the season. If you only have ninety minutes, adjust accordingly. The following plan is a tight one. Players need to hustle from drill to drill. Coaching should be crisp. Nearly everything is done at top speed. Monitor the pace and give a breather here or there as needed.

On the last page of this chapter is a blank practice plan that you can copy. You can waste a lot of time if you are not organized, but you can triple the value of the practice if you are.

First Weeks of Preseason: Daily Practice Schedule

Early birds run laps: forward, backward, shuffle. Jumping and vertical-leap drills. Foul shots, individual-moves work. Vision-therapy drills can be demonstrated and suggested for further use at home.

Conditioning 6:00 P.M. Quick cali set, a few from the-leg stretch set.

Speed drills: robot, bounce, buttkick, goosestep (do one or two).
Agility drills: simon-says or carioca.
Jumping drills.

Call Team Together 6:20 P.M. Brief comments.

Stations, Skills Practice 6:25 P.M. Set up six stations, two drills each on dribbling, passing, and rebounding. Rotate every four minutes. It will take longer at first to set up the stations, but after a few practices, it can move very quickly.

Occasionally, devote this skills period to just *position* or *shooting* stations, as described previously. Use drills such as 21-jumper, 21-lay-up and 50-freebies. Have players shoot from their optimum location. Each player needs to find and know their range and slowly extend it. Remind them they need to practice shots on their own generally, but you need to conduct drills at practice so you can observe their form.

Water Break 6:50 P.M.

151

Defensive Skills Practice 7:00 P.M. Coach demonstrates triple-threat form, deny-pass and fronting form (low and high post), and rebound/boxing form. Then splits the players into two groups. Do the no-arm -shuffle and three-man-rebound drills. At another practice, do the rip the screen and drop-step drills. After a week or two, introduce the three-on-two-on-one.

Offensive Skills Practice 7:30 P.M. Each day coaches demonstrate one or two areas of form: triple-threat offensive form, jump-shot form (particularly jump straight and high, cradle high, wrist form), dribbling form, passing form, boxing out form, lay-up form. Then break players into two groups and do a few drills dedicated to that subject, and areas previously covered.

Sprints, Races, "Suicides." 7:50 P.M.

Closing Comments, Practice Over 8:00 P.M.

Post-Practice: Foul shots until parent comes.

Midway Between First Practice and First Game: Saturday Practice Schedule

Early birds run laps: forward, backward, shuffle. Jumping and vertical-leap drills. Foul shots, individual-moves work.

Conditioning 11:00 A.M. Quick cali set, leg-stretch set.

> Speed Drills: robot, bounce, buttkick, goosestep. Have players do two of each. Jumping Drills.

Call Team Together 11:10 A.M. Brief comments.

Defensive Skills Practice 11:15 A.M. Split players into two groups at either end. Each group does one drill, no-arm-shuffle, three-man-rebound, or three-on-two-on-one for ten minutes. Observe form fundamentals; use checklist.

Water Break 11:30 A.M.

Offensive Skills Practice 11:40 A.M. Split into two groups, do crisscross drill, around the world, stop-pivot-go drill.

Shooting Practice 12:00 P.M. Drills such as 21-jumper, 21-lay-up, and 50-freebies. Post players do medley or rapid shooting drill. Let players focus on their best shot, and take a step beyond their range to see how it's improving.

Water Break 12:20 P.M.

Team Practice 12:25 P.M. Break the squad up into two even teams. Walk through a play pattern (e.g., shuffle, wheel, pick and roll). Slowly have the players apply light defense, using no arms at first; in a day or so, increase gradually to full defense.

Every other day, introduce one specialty drill, such as inbounding (under your hoop, sideline, under their hoop), center tap, fast break, breaking the press.

Scrimmage 1:00 P.M. Be sure players not involved in the scrimmage are working on something useful.

Closing Comments, Practice Over 1:20 P.M.

Post Practice: Foul shots until parent comes.

Mid-Season: Daily Practice Schedule

Early birds run laps: forward, backward, shuffle. Jumping and vertical-leap drills. Foul shots, individual-moves work.

Conditioning 6:00 P.M. Quick cali set, leg-stretch set.

Jumping Drills.

Call Team Together 6:10 P.M. Brief comments.

Stations 6:15 P.M. Use stations to address weaknesses you've seen or to sharpen individual skills. If someone is dropping passes, have him do receiving drills. If the team is lax on boxing out, do those drills.

Shooting Practice 6:40 P.M. Have team do drills such as 21-jumper, 21-lay-up, and 50-freebies. Let players focus on their best shot, and take a step beyond their range to see how it's improving.

Water Break 6:55 P.M.

Scrimmage 7:05 P.M. First team against subs. Practice. Run the offense. Stop play when mental errors are made.

Sprints, Races, "Suicides," Foul Shots 7:45 P.M.

Closing Comments, Practice Over 7:55 P.M.

Post-Practice: Foul shots until parent comes.

09

THE PSYCHOLOGY OF COACHING

Aren't they too young to learn all this? Will the competition, the emphasis on winning, be too much at certain ages or for certain types of kids? How do you motivate a rambunctious ten-year-old? How do you get kids to play with consistency? What is a good age to start? The answers to these questions depend a lot on what the coach is looking for out of her coaching experience. Is it about winning, teaching?

I define coaching as the art of *inspiring* a child to draw something greater from themselves in the effort to succeed. The rest flows from there.

DON'T UNDERESTIMATE YOUR PLAYERS

If your players—or your son or daughter—are very young (less than nine), then it will be a few years before they understand the more technical parts of the game well enough to routinely put it together on the court. But all of it, including the more complicated concepts such as continuous patterns, pick and roll, fast break should be taught, or at least introduced, at all ages. Don't underestimate your players. Some of them will grasp these concepts. The basics, especially dribbling, passing, screening, and shooting, should be emphasized right away, before bad habits form. However, a lot of the refinements, such as defending the screen, multiple fakes, and posting up take time and maturity.

IT TAKES TIME AND PATIENCE

Believe me when I say there is no magic age that you should expect kids to learn complex skills. Look at kids mastering moves in gymnastics, soccer, and other sports at seven and eight years old. It's not that younger kids can't learn. They just need someone who understands refined concepts and has the time and ability to teach them.

How quickly they learn largely depends on how much time you have to practice, and, unfortunately, that's the biggest problem. We all have many obligations, and youth

154

sports usually can't be practiced every day. Do what you can. There isn't anything in this book that's over their heads. Just start somewhere, and the kids will absorb as much as you have the time and patience to teach them.

Some skills will take a few sessions; some require much more; and some will take years, but it will happen. Like learning how to ride a bike, suddenly one day the kids can do it, and they then understand it was always really simple to do.

THE COACH-PLAYER RELATIONSHIP

The relationship between a coach and a player is a powerful one. You are not only a father or mother figure, but you are the final authority in what is, in the player's mind, the most important thing in life.

Through his athletic experiences, a kid finds out things about himself—good or bad—and he will always associate those things with you. Coaching is an awesome responsibility. You may want to ignore this larger picture, but sticking your head in the sand does not change what's really going on. This book provides many tools you can use to help you make the experience a good one, whether you win or lose as a team, but in the final analysis, it comes down to whether you really care enough and are secure enough to accept the larger role of being both a coach and a friend.

Most of your players will never make cuts at the high-school level, only a few may play in college, and you will probably never coach a future professional basketball player. However, every one of your players will become an adult someday, with the responsibility of a job and probably a family as well. The whole idea of youth sports is to provide life lessons. It is doubtful that players will remember much about the season twenty years from now, certainly not the scores of various games. I guarantee you one thing, though: They will remember you for the rest of their lives. The memory of my coaches is etched clearly in my mind. I remember them vividly, for good or for bad. You may not remember all the kids you coached, particularly if you do it for a number of years, but every one of them will remember you. How do you want to be remembered?

ON WINNING

"Our society is ferociously competitive in spirit. Pressuring children too hard may turn them into adults so obsessed with being first that they get no joy out of life except in the narrow field of competition. They neither give nor get pleasure in their relationships with spouses, children, friends, and fellow workers."

—Dr. Benjamin Spock

155

> "Basketball is like a war! ... Winning comes first!
>
> *—Red Auerbach, Former Coach, General Manager, President, Boston Celtics*

Feelings on the importance of winning run strong. As with religion and politics, everyone thinks they are right. Vince Lombardi, the legendary coach of the Packers football team, once said, "Winning isn't everything...it's the only thing." There are still coaches who will tell you that, if you are going to keep score, you should try to win.

Let's face it, if you tell kids winning is no big deal, they may blankly nod, but I guarantee they won't buy it. They know all about winning. They know the guys on the other team will gloat and taunt them back at school. They know about medallions, trophies, and news articles. They *hear* the empty silence after a loss, the lectures from the coach: They feel the pressure.

Well, the truth is somewhere in between. Kids talk about winning, but I believe that, down deep, they care as much or even more about how well they are doing personally. Many of you will remember, from your playing days, a game where the team won, but you didn't contribute. Was that satisfactory? Or how about a game where the team lost, but you had a super day? How did you feel? Sure you wanted to win. Sure it's a team sport. But the personal satisfaction went a long way toward easing the pain.

All right, winning is important in the pros. Maybe it becomes important even for some kids in high school, since scholarship money rarely looks at anybody on a team with a 3-and-26 record. In youth basketball, however, it's just not important. Parents and coaches may think it is, but the kids often forget the game, and certainly the score, as soon as they get to the ice cream stand.

What they will remember, however, is how they feel about themselves and how you reacted. Want practical advice? I tell my kids something they can believe, that winning is never important in youth basketball, but that it is always fun to win. That's the truth. They can relate to it. I tell them that what's important is how they handle victory or defeat; that it's important to try to be as good as they can be, to help each other, and to try to do their best. We try to win, but all we can really control is how hard we try.

BALANCE THE NEED TO WIN

At the heart of how good a coach you will be is how well you balance the need to win with the need to develop healthy young people. This balance will affect your every action, your relationship with each player, and the atmosphere on the court. It will characterize the memory of your coaching experience for many years to come. Striking that balance involves a continuing struggle between the passions fired up by competition and the caring you feel for your players as a responsible adult. A basketball game will stir up some powerful emotions. It's said that winning builds character, while losing reveals it. Competitive fire can quickly melt an otherwise cool, calm, collected attitude.

How to Find Your Balance

I often found my own balance in light of how much talent we had on the team. When I saw we had little chance of winning it all, I chose to emphasize individual goals. Let's face it, if you can't get there, there is absolutely no sense in getting everyone crazy. But when you have the potential championship team—that's a bit different!

The point is, it *is* a balance. Winning and development are both part of the game. For instance, we may worry about the total dedication required of young Olympic athletes, having sacrificed much of their youth for their quest. Yet we know they have enjoyed moments of glory which seem to transcend life itself, achieving heights most of us only dream about.

At beginner levels, winning is simply never important. At intermediate and advanced levels, again, player development is always important, but, in those few instances when the team has a good chance to win a championship, then winning is an appropriate team goal. This means perhaps more practice, playing the better kids a bit more, raising competitive spirits a bit higher. Talk about where the team is and agree to go for it, as a team.

COMPETITION: PART OF LIFE?

It's just not realistic and certainly not helpful to have "experts" like Alfie Kohn tell us in his book *No Contest: The Case Against Competition* (Houghton Mifflin) that years of psychological research prove "competition is poison." That is like telling us not to breathe because the air is polluted! Competition is a part of life, period!

I don't think the proper balance was found by Eric Margenau, a renowned sports psychologist who, in *Sports Without Pressure: A Guide for Parents and Coaches of Young Parents* (Gardner Press, 1990), suggested that "Competition is fine, but should be kept friendly … Parents should not pressure a child to excel regardless of that child's abilities." I disagree. Let's face it: We all know kids who could excel but don't, and need a good nudge to get going.

By the same token, many of us will remember the ugly scene on national TV, when irresistible competitive fires drove Ohio State coaching legend Woody Hayes to assault an opposing Clemson player on the field. And we cringed when young tennis star Mary Pierce, symbolic of many troubled young athletes, had to obtain a restraining order against her father, who had been pressuring her. The frenzy to win, riding upon the dark horse of fear of failure, can and does get both crazy and destructive.

157

The issue of competition goes to the essence of the human condition: It is part of our evolution. Its answers are complex and most elusive. After many years of coaching and playing sports, to me the clearest answer is to not give up. I read years ago in the New York Times that some schools are abandoning competitive interaction in their physical-education programs to avoid damaging the feelings of kids who are not outstanding. Isn't it better that kids learn about and prepare for success and failure in a controlled setting, inside a relatively harmless gymnasium, rather than face it for the first time in the crucible of adult life? Can't we, as a society, learn how to prepare children to be confident, self-assured, and focused, to learn that sometimes you succeed and sometimes you don't, and to do so in a friendly non-threatening environment?

Should we abandon competition, and with it, the struggle to succeed, just because we, as a society, haven't completely figured out how to do it right? We couldn't quit if we wanted to. It's part of life, and we must continue to work to find the best balance.

WINNING AND GROWTH

Winning and growth do share a common ground. Coaches who win consistently are often remembered by their former players more for the great lessons of life, than for the gold cup on the mantle.

These coaches know that the key to success is in motivating athletes to win their personal struggles, to do their best, not to quit, and to find within themselves resources beyond their apparent limitations. They motivate by combining personal goals with the team's goals. These coaches know that the spirit, the will to win, and the will to excel are the important things that transcend the game itself.

How you resolve the balance between winning and individual development is up to you. If you recognize the need to strike a balance, you are off to a good start. My own approach in coaching is probably best characterized as a back-and-forth struggle to maintain that balance. When I find myself too focused on the win, when I feel those natural emotions churning, I step back a bit. I remind myself that, while we're going for it, we need to stay on the high road.

Every coach has felt the gut-wrenching feeling that stays with you for hours after a game. I think it's enough to be honest about the reality of competitive passion, and then commit yourself to doing what you expect of your players—doing your best with it!

I believe most coaches want to build character and create a positive experience for each player, and they want to win the game. There are some coaches who never really challenge their teams for fear of upsetting the kids, and these "nice guys" don't do much damage. Of course, their players may never make it to the next level of play. Other coaches feel compelled to win at any cost, and the cost can be tragic for the fragile psyche of a young child.

158

Find the middle ground. If you can't deal with the pressure, then consider whether coaching is right for you (or for the kids).

USE REALITY CHECKS

Parents talk to each other about how they feel and how their kids are feeling. One practical way to get a "reality check" is to pick out a parent who seems to know the other parents well and ask her how the parents think things are going. She may offer insight into general problems or even problems related to a specific child that no other parent would ever tell you directly.

Of course, the balance between winning and building character seems to vary with the age of your team. So be realistic. At preteen levels, the most emphasis is usually placed on developing the individual. This doesn't mean that winning is not an issue: It's just not at all important. The focus is on development. This is why most programs require that all kids play a minimal amount of time. By high-school varsity play, the balance between winning and growth becomes more even. It should never get further than that, but the reality of major collegiate play is that losing coaches don't last.

ON MOTIVATION

> "Rock, I know I'm going to die. I'm not afraid. But someday, Rock, when things on the field are going against us, tell the boys, Rock, to go out there and win just one for the Gipper. Now, I know where I'll be then, coach. But I'll know about it, and I'll be happy."
>
> —*George Gipp*

OK, it's a football story, but it's the best motivation story there is. Legendary Notre Dame coach Knute Rockne waited eight years until, during halftime in a big game against Army, he repeated these last words of his dying quarterback in what was to become the epitome of halftime motivation.

It's a beautiful story, but coaches need to rely upon a lot more than speeches to motivate their team. Sure, some coaches have that charismatic quality and can motivate a team just by the sheer strength of their personality.

However, the rest of us "mere-mortal" guys need to consider motivational techniques that can help us get the job done. The "secrets" of good motivation are easily found in the growing science of sports psychology. Once considered mere gobbledygook, the mental aspect of competition is now a cornerstone of athletic development at the highest levels of amateur and professional sports. Many team organizations, including the U.S. Olympic program, have employed full-time sports psychologists.

159

It is not the purpose of this book to go into the psychology of sports in great depth. You will find aspects of psychology spread throughout this book, as well as in my books on coaching other youth sports. I have used psychological insight throughout my twenty years of coaching, and you will probably agree that much of this is common sense, obvious to any caring adult. My checklist approach to teaching correct form is consistent with the mental checklist sports psychologists urge athletes to use. If you want to focus more deeply on this area, one of the best books I've read on this subject is *The Athlete's Guide to Sports Psychology: Mental Skills for Physical People* by Dorothy V. Harris, Ph.D. and Bette L. Harris, Ed.D. (Leisure Press, 1984). I will, however, discuss some emerging motivational techniques that seem to work best.

ATTABOY!

There never will be a better tool than frequent positive reinforcement for young athletes. It is essential to liberally give out some attaboys (or attagirls) for good effort.

In *Kidsports: A Survival Guide for Parents* (Addison-Wesley, 1983), Dr. Nathan J. Smith, a consultant for the American Board of Pediatrics, studied two groups of coaches. He found that "the single most important difference in our research between coaches to whom young athletes respond most favorably and those to whom they respond least favorably was the frequency with which coaches reinforce and reward desirable behavior."

A pat on the back, a smile, clapping, praise, a wink and a nod, as well as tangible rewards such as mention in a newspaper article or more playing time—all go a very long way toward motivating high performance. I would add to this concept that the rewards are even more effective when they emphasize outstanding effort as opposed to a great result. An athlete has complete control over the amount of effort he puts into his game. The result, however, is dependent on many things, many of which are beyond the individual's control. Even corrective action, pointing out mistakes, should be sandwiched somehow within some positive comments; e.g., "Good try, Jack. Next time get a better shot—you can do it!"

FUGGEDDABOUTIT!!!

Kids need to know that they will lose sometimes, and so it's useful to talk about it and point out that, at youth levels, the only important thing is learning. Point out that some kids get an edge from more experience or earlier physical development, and by high school we all largely catch up. The key is for the kids to understand that losing and learn-

MOTIVATIONAL PHRASES

SHOOTING

Front of the rim.

Soft hands.

Square to the basket.

Get a good shot.

Shoot with confidence.

Stick it.

Get up.

DEFENSE

Hands up.

Get the ball.

Pressure.

Get wide.

Nothing past you.

Stay low.

Everything.

AFTER A BAD PLAY

Relax.

Learn from it.

Shake it off.

We'll get it back.

Get a better shot.

Think.

Come back.

AFTER A LOSS

Was it your best effort?

Use your teammates.

How much do you want it?

We've got to pass better.

We need to shoot smarter.

We're better than this.

Let's focus more next time.

AFTER A WIN

It was a team win.

Super effort.

It's happening.

That's basketball.

You earned it.

Don't gloat.

Just smile.

ing are the same things, it's just another learning experience. The only thing important is for the kids to do their best and get better. When the loss occurs, remind them of these things ... winning is fun, but what we are learning is all that matters now!

DON'T BE A COACH WHO LOSES IT

Some coaches spend a lot of time hollering, trying to motivate players, trying to get them to increase their energy level and to develop that all-important desire to perform. However, we often see these coaches just lose it and cross the line of tolerable motivation. In the face of poor performance, the better approach is to be firm, to let players know they can do better if they reach deeper in their gut. I like to ask players if they gave it their best. "Was that your best effort?" "Can you do better?"

FOCUS ON THE EFFORT

Let a player know what you think about his effort, but don't personalize it—the kid is a decent person. Focus on the effort during practice. A kid can relate to trying harder, but he can't relate to you telling him he stinks.

Explain the problem with fundamentals or form, so he understands the concept. Take the time he needs to get the idea. Most importantly, reward good effort openly and liberally. Praise a good steal. Recognize hustle. Yell out, "That's basketball!" It can get infectious. Especially at beginner levels, but through intermediate levels as well, your comments should always be in a calm, low tone and should be constructive. At these levels, the kids just don't have the skills, and all the yelling in the world won't improve skills.

Having one set of standards for everyone doesn't mean you shouldn't handle players differently. Some kids respond well when you correct them in from of their peers. Others are devastated when you get on them, even if done calmly. You will quickly get a feel for this from their reaction to you. Take these kids aside, and explain what you saw. Some kids will seem troubled all the time, so sit down with them and find out what's going on in their lives; see if you can learn what the problem is.

In chapter one, we discussed the differences between girls and boys in motivation, but I doubt there is any difference in how boys or girls want to be treated; and screaming is just *never* helpful.

At advanced levels, your expectations for performance are much higher. Players will generally have the skills, and it is the lapses in concentration which most affect performance. A coach may firmly and constructively criticize a player, but he must always use a controlled tone. Yelling will get a kid's attention, but it will also humiliate him. There is a way to get their attention and still be positive. As noted earlier, the essence of coaching is to inspire an athlete to be all they can be, so coaching criticism must be grounded in the notion that the player can do better.

WE ARE FAMILY!

I've read the autobiographies of many great coaches. One constant in all their stories is their ability to relate to the different individuals on their team, to create a family-type environment. Each kid is different, and each one needs a personal approach. Most importantly, even the last substitute should be treated with equal respect to the starting players.

I start each season with a team discussion on what it means to be on a team. One thing I tell the players is that, for the rest of the season, they are all friends. They are all in a special relationship with each other. I tell them they should say hello in the school hallways, and help each other off the court, if needed. I never tolerate criticism of a teammate on the court and I quickly bench any offender. Kids are expected to urge each other on, to quickly tell a teammate to put a mistake behind him. I promote team dinners and outings, and I move to break up cliques.

Team-building is a proven ticket to success. The concept is widely used in all walks of life, and it is a staple of Japanese and American business organization. It doesn't just happen because a bunch of kids are on a team. It happens when coaches work at it. Team-building is actually quite easy to get done; just put it in the practice plan. Talk to your assistant coaches about it, and opportunities to promote team unity will present themselves in abundance. There are many ways to build team spirit. A pizza party early on will allow an opportunity for everyone to get to know on another better, and it also lets you get some concepts across. Team parties at the end of the season, with awards or some kind of parting trophy, are nice to let kids know that, no matter how the season ended, they succeeded.

SET REALISTIC GOALS

It may seem trite to say, but setting realistic goals is essential to proper motivation for the team and for each individual. With specific goals, a kid has something clear and achievable to work on, something she can set her sights on. She is not responsible for the whole team, nor for winning or losing. She is not overwhelmed and defeated by unrealistic expectations.

I think it's a good idea to have each player set his own goals under your guidance. I usually offer the players a number of categories in which a few goals should be set.

One category is conditioning, and the goals may be to double the number of pushups he can do, knock a few seconds off a 100-yard sprint, or increase the number of pull-ups.

A second goal category relates to specific skills a player's his position. The goal may be to improve the form of his shot or his defensive stance.

A third goal category relates to game performance, for example, the number of rebounds. I might also suggest to a player that she work on her self-confidence, her self-control, her relationship with certain teammates, or her effort at practice. The player writes this down, and we'll occasionally review progress. Don't set too many goals; just focus on key areas.

ON PEAK PERFORMANCE

The bane of coaches is whatever it is that makes a kid play great one day and completely fall apart the next. A kid misses his first five shots, and he winds up walking around in a daze all day. Another kid makes a good steal, and he suddenly starts to terrorize the court. One day, the guard can't pass to save his life. Other days, his play seems transcendent.

THE FIGHT OR FLIGHT INSTINCT

Modern science tells us that how we cope with the stress of the challenge is all "upstairs," at least much of it. Mental control, or its lack, begins with the commonly known "fight or flight" instinct—the natural impulse that arises in cornered animals to respond to a threat by fighting it or fleeing from it. It is a genetic reaction, which, as humans, we inherited from our earliest ancient ancestors.

There's not a kid alive who hasn't felt those butterflies in the stomach. This reaction under game conditions can create a panic that distracts concentration and may even cause muscle spasms. However, when controlled properly, it can lead the athlete to a "zone" of peak performance.

STUDIES EXPLAIN WHAT HAPPENS

In the February 14, 1994, issue of *U.S. News and World Report*, an article entitled "The Inner Game of Winning" reported on the research of Stanford University neurobiologist Robert Sapolsky. He found that a properly controlled response to challenge causes a desirable increase in adrenaline and sugar, producing the sense of "heightened awareness and flow" associated with being in a peak "zone." The negative counterpart, which he calls the "fearful" response, produces a body cocktail laced with a substance called cortisol, which can "not only impair performance, but can also lead over the long run to damage the arteries and liver and lead to depression."

Another interesting study, "The Mental Edge: The Brain Is the Key to Peak Performance in Sports and Life," appeared in the August 3, 1992 issue of the same magazine. Brian Hatfield of the University of Maryland reported that at moments of peak performance, the brain's left side, the analytic side, erupts in a burst of relaxing alpha waves, indicative of a relaxed, trancelike state. This allows the right side of the brain, which controls spatial relations and pattern recognition, to control the body.

Okay, what do these studies have to do with kids playing basketball? They help us understand and correct inconsistencies. Research suggests several steps you can take to create or strive for the conditions optimal to peak performance.

BREATHE DEEPLY

Perhaps the greatest control of game-day jitters is deep breathing. Have your players inhale deeply for two seconds, hold their breath for eight seconds, and exhale for four seconds. This can also be done while alternatively closing each nostril, breathing in one nostril, out the other. It is a great relaxation technique and has been a staple of yoga for thousands of years.

REPETITION, REPETITION, REPETITION

The best way to produce a controlled response to game-day excitement is constant repetition during practice. Much of this book deals with the need to repeatedly practice dribbling and shooting, including adherence to proper form. Players need to do this so the game responses become automatic and so they can occur even if the player is under stress or too excited.

FOLLOW A GAME-DAY PATTERN

Both studies also suggest that a ritual-like approach to game day is conducive to the relaxed state of mind needed. A regular pattern of eating, exercise, dressing, and pre-game discussion is highly recommended. Try to avoid any surprises or deviations. The present mental routine should apply right up to the opening buzzer.

PREPARE THE MIND, VISUALIZATIONS

Tell kids that they need to prepare the mind as well as the body if they are to reach their best potential. Encourage them to run through a checklist of form (e.g., hands up, eye on the ball, stay low, follow through with the gooseneck). Tell them to mentally picture the play, imagine themselves with great form stealing the ball and driving to the hoop. This stuff works and is well accepted at the highest levels of sport. Sports psychologists have anticipated current research findings in their long-time support of mental imaging of athletic routines. Olympic athletes have been tracing their steps mentally for years. Now we have clear scientific bases for this approach.

RELAX, DON'T LET THE ADRENALINE BUILD UP TOO EARLY

Sapolsky notes that premature arousal of adrenaline hours before the game can result in the adrenaline level in the blood dropping after a few hours, even to a point below normal at game time. This will lead to subpart performance and is another reason to have relaxed, stable pregame routines. Many coaches now employ Zen-type meditations in the training programs, providing athletes with methods to evoke relaxed states of mind at will.

USE THESE TECHNIQUES AT ALL LEVELS

Control techniques are useful at all levels of play. They are perhaps most needed at the youngest levels, when kids cannot control the anxieties of competition. Relaxed game-day rituals, mental imaging, affirmations of self-esteem, review of checklists (such as contained in chapter twelve), are techniques that can be repeatedly practiced.

GET AN EDGE

Many coaches have some concept they use to focus players on achieving peak performance. I always told my players to try to get an edge over their opponent. We talked about how evenly matched most good teams usually are and that the winner would be the team who got some kind of edge over the opponent.

This concept helped me to get kids to accept, for instance, the idea of improving their mental approach—as one way to get an edge. I would tell kids to double the number of pushups they could do, since the other kids on other teams probably weren't doing it, and so they would get a bit stronger than them.

ON PARENTS

As you know, parents can be a great help in youth sports; however, interfering parents can be a major problem for coaches. This is especially true in indoor sports like basketball because parents are usually right on top of the team, so their complaining is more visible.

I have no problem with parents who, after the game, want to talk to the coach and find out whether there is some problem they need to be aware of. Often, however, they are argumentative and sometimes downright insulting.

Of course, you don't need to take abuse from any parent. Before you get too defensive, however, think about what's going on.

PARENTS FEEL FOR THEIR KIDS

Most parents die a little bit when they see their child going through a bad time. Maybe their daughter is not playing much, having self-doubts, and acting out because of it. Parents feel the pain along with their kids—it's tough for anyone to feel she's not good enough.

OFFER SUGGESTIONS

Hear parents out. Give them some ideas to help understand what the problem is, and perhaps you can focus them on things they can do to help at home. Talk about drills that can be done at home to improve performance. Tell them you think their child can do better, and you are trying to arouse his potential. Maybe, in return, you can get some insight into what is troubling the child. Maybe, just maybe, you are dead wrong, and you need to give the kid another look. Tell the parents you will do that. I've seen kids sit on the bench as a substitute for half a season, suddenly come alive, and become starters.

BE UNDERSTANDING

Most of all, keep in mind that he's their kid! They may feel a bit threatened by your control over their child. As a parent, I have had uneasy feelings about coaches: It's quite natural. A little patience on your part can defuse some strong emotions. You can turn a potential feud into something that helps the child and, ultimately, the team. Try it.

DON'T TOLERATE ABUSE

A major problem is the parent who abuses his child during a game. He scorns his son or daughter for missing a shot or for bad defense. It's the worst thing in sports to see. You do not have to put up with this. Talk to the parent and ask him to keep quiet. If he doesn't, remove him from the gym. Once, while I was coaching baseball, one parent threatened me with removing his son as well. My response was merely that I hoped he wouldn't, but that not playing was probably better than what was going on and that it would not continue under my watch. The parent stayed home; the kid played.

EMPOWER PARENTS

Frankly, I rarely had problems with parents. When you achieve a certain level of team spirit, it becomes infectious, and negativity gets left behind. I always sought to empower parents, get them involved with the team in some manner: as coaches, as drill monitors, in charge of water breaks, fund drives, uniforms, or phone trees. Delegate as much as possible, and you'll bring parents into the team dynamic. I would try to avoid having a parent coach his own child at practice, if possible, and this pertains to the head coach as well. Each season, I'd ask my assistant coach to agree that we'd each focus on each other's kid as much as possible. Kids hear their parents differently than another adult; they react differently.

Chapter eight points out ways parents can help keep more activity going on in practice. They can rebound for shooting practice, provide light dummy defense, coach their kids at home. Push gently to get them involved, but don't push too hard.

SOME NOTES FOR PARENTS

Parents would be wise to follow these guidelines:

1. Evaluate Your Child's Potential and Desire, and Be Honest. If your child is a beginner, the first objective is for him to learn the game fundamentals. Go over terminology and concepts. Take him to a high-school, college, or pro game. Sign him up for a clinic. Start by promoting dribbling, lay-ups, and short jump shots.

2. As Your Child Improves, Begin to Add More Challenges During Your Practice Sessions. Don't dominate your child. (I used to defend against my sons initially without using my hands.) Increase pressure as she can take it; challenge her. Begin to introduce other concepts—give and go, pick and roll, screening, stealing the ball, rebounding. As short jumpers are mastered, move farther out. Practice foul shots.

3. As Your Child Becomes a Decent Player, You Can Help by Concentrating on Specific Skills. If he's tall, give him low-post practice while you defend, again, only aggressively enough to make it a challenge. Forwards should shoot from the corners and wing and practice baseline drives. Guards needs to practice speed dribbling, so apply open-court defensive pressure. Practice snappy passing and outside shooting from above the high post. Set goals to improve free-throw percentage. If he can only make three out of twenty, work to get it to five, seven, ten, and fifteen. If he is in grade school, you may have to move him in a bit to find a good range, then slowly move him back to the line. There are basketball camps available in most states, and some clubs employ personal trainers or experts to run clinics for the kids. These are usually helpful, but the best prescription is to play a lot.

4. Encourage Your Daughter to Play if She Wants to Play. Basketball is popular for both boys and girls, and the girls' teams are growing rapidly. It seems to me, when viewing girls' games, that girls don't spend as much time shooting as boys do. Their shot percentages are much lower when they are young. If your daughter is interested in playing, concentrate on jump shots—she can be a star very quickly.

HOW CAN YOU GET YOUR CHILD INTERESTED IN SPORTS?

The most important thing is to avoid the negative stuff, as I have repeated often in this book. If your child is afraid of competition, fearful of being embarrassed, or tired of your impatience (if you are yelling at her and getting annoyed or frustrated), she will never be interested. Perhaps sports are just not for her, and you need to let her pursue other interests. Some parents have a hard time accepting that.

But if she's just anxious about playing, or if she is unsure, help her to get over it. Tell her there is an athlete somewhere inside her, and you are going to work with her to develop it. Communicate. Discuss the things in this book—talk basketball, go to a pro game or to a local high-school game. Watch games on TV; work with your child in trying to collect a whole series of basketball cards. If you go out and coach her and she gets better, you won't have to worry about interest.

Many afternoons I got home from work, and my sons were on the stoop with a basketball. The court was across the street. "Hey Dad, you ready to play?" Interest? I couldn't turn it off. We became buddies through sports. You work closely with your child on something like this, and she will not only be interested in basketball, she'll become interested in you. How can you lose?

PARENTAL BEHAVIOR AT GAMES

I'm not going to tell you to reduce your energy and just sit there and be quiet. However, if you read this book carefully, you'll know how to act at games.

First, don't pressure your child, or anyone else's. Be particularly cautious about criticizing a player on the other team; a parent or friend may be near by and confrontation can easily arise. Second, say intelligent, helpful things like "get the ball," "make it happen," "pressure," "in their faces,"—things that will help him remember the basics. Study the list of motivational phrases on page 161 for encouraging words to call out. Be positive.

At games, get to know the other parents. It's really a beautiful thing when a team becomes one big family. Most of mine have been that way because I promote it as a high priority. It makes everything more loose, more relaxed, and that's better for the kids. It can also lead to some rewarding friendships and to a deeper feeling of communication, and that's icing on the cake. In addition, you might get another parent interested in helping his son, and that's super. Finally, suggest they read this book.

Perhaps the ugliest spectacle at youth basketball games is parental abuse of referees. The seats are usually close to the action, and frustrations and anxiety far too often translate into yelling at the ref. I can tell you from experience that refereeing basketball games is the toughest referee job there is. Things move very quickly, and often a call is made with just a good guess. Rise above this type of behavior; it will just increase your anxiety and could lead to your doing something you will regret. Stay in control and leave the referee alone.

HOW TO DEAL WITH THE COACH

I hope you will have read this book and practiced with your child before you even meet your child's first coach. Then you can offer your help as an assistant or even sign up for the top job. At six to eight years old, there is not much skill on the court to worry about, and it is a good starting place for inexperienced coaches.

Learn About the Coach

I recommend you ask around about the coach's reputation. Find out about her from parents whose kids had her the year before. Did she play all the kids each game? Did she lose her temper? Did she conduct practices on time? Most coaches are fine; some will be better teachers than others, but a few are not good for your child, and you can find out early and consider whether it's best for your child to play for that person.

Get Involved

I suggest you find some way to get involved. When the coach calls, offer whatever help you can give. If your job takes up your weekdays, offer to help on weekends. Many coaches will be happy for it. Some don't want help, so there's not much you can do, but you can still work with your child at home.

Some parents just like to sit and watch practice. I don't mind; most coaches won't either. Besides, it will help you become aware of areas where your child can use improvement.

Fairness is a Two-Way Street

If your child is playing the minimum, but only the minimum, be fair before you approach the coach. Usually, coaches are out to win, and they do play the best players. Help your child work a little harder, and he may improve enough to play more.

If the coach is being unfair, talk to him about it. It is a difficult thing for all involved. Don't get mad. The coach could take it out on your child. Don't duck the problem either. A few questions to the coach, nicely stated, will help, such as, "What can Johnny do to get more playing time?"

If the coach is a negative person (you will probably get one for your child at some point), you may need to let the local board know about it. Bad coaches need to be weeded out. They can do a lot of damage.

YOUR PLAYERS' HEALTH 10

CONDITIONING

I rarely recommend weight training for youth sports, and I certainly don't do so for basketball. I'll discuss this further, later in this section. A good stretching and calisthenics program is adequate, and I provide a list of exercises in chapter eight. Pushups on the fingertips are the best exercise, since forearm and wrist strength is important in basketball. Tell your players to do what they can, and, over time, to work up to thirty to fifty per day. Chin-ups, as many as the player can do, are also quite helpful. Wrist, forearm, and shoulder strength are very important to upper-body strength, and any help that you can give here will be immediately and quite noticeably rewarded on the court. I got my son a set of chest expanders, with springs attached to handles, and he used to do them while watching cartoons. The wrist machine mentioned in chapter eight is great for home practice. I always had one in my duffle bag, and the kids used it after shooting practice. Rowing exercises are also very good to increase strength and stamina.

As, or more, important than the arms and upper body in basketball are the legs. Wind sprints are the best leg exercise. Partial squats, bending the knee halfway with some extra weight added, are quite good. The kids shouldn't bend all the way. The long-standing tradition of running up stairs is excellent. Jumping exercises are great.

Stretching before practice and before games will help prevent muscles from tearing or snapping. No practice of any kind should begin without some slow jogging, some jumping jacks (for the ankles), and some general stretching (for the upper thigh, trunk, and neck). Running sideways and backward, or doing any agility exercises, are quite good also.

Warming up muscles by stretching, lay-ups, and agility exercises is needed at all levels of play, for both boys and girls. The session can be shorter for beginners, as the practice plans in chapter eight suggest. Conditioning, to gain strength, is probably even less important at beginner or intermediate levels for basketball but should be urged at

171

more advanced levels, certainly by high school. There is one exception at grade-school levels: Kids generally lack the strength to shoot with one hand beyond seven to ten feet from the hoop, and pushups address that issue directly. Girls tend to have even less upper-body strength, so pushups are even more important for them.

As noted, I generally believe that weight training should be avoided by grade-school level players and not started until mid-high-school years. Part of the reason is intuitive: A child's body is growing rapidly until then, and studies suggest that there is significant risk of injury to kids' growth plates, which are the ends of the long bones that account for growth.

A careful study of 354 high-school football players by Dr. William Risser of the University of Texas Medical School found that weight lifting can cause severe musculoskeletal injuries, usually muscle strains, and often in the lower back. 7.1 percent of the players reported injury. Injuries occurred when free weights were used in major lifts, such as the clean and jerk, the snatch, the squat lift, the dead lift, the power clean, and the bench, incline, and overhead presses. Most injuries occurred in the home and were related to poor technique and form, lack of warm-up, and lack of a spotter to assist.

However, I must report that research suggests a different point of view from my own. In the November 1990 issue of Pediatrics (Vol. 86, No. 5), the American Academy of Pediatrics Committee on Sports Medicine and Fitness said, "Recent research has shown that short-term programs in which prepubescent [grade-school] athletes are trained and supervised by knowledgeable adults can increase strength without significant training as a conditioning method for participants in male and female sports. The major lifts are often used … Strength training in adolescence occasionally produces significant musculoskeletal injury … especially during use of the major lifts. Safety requires careful planning of several aspects of a program. This includes devising a program for the intensity, duration, frequency, and rate of progression of weight use, as well as selection of sport-specific exercises appropriate for the physical maturity of the individual. Proper supervision should be provided during training sessions." The committee also addressed the issue of when kids should be allowed to lift maximal amounts of weight, that is, the greatest amount of weight they can successfully lift. They concluded that this should be avoided until kids have passed their period of maximal velocity of height growth. Young people of both sexes reach that state, on average, at age fifteen, but the committee also notes that there is "much individual variation." Consequently, based on the contents of this article, the American Academy of Pediatrics recommends that each child's state of physical maturity be assessed by medical personnel and that the adults planning strength-training programs be qualified to develop programs appropriate for varying stages of maturity.

Another good article, "Strength Training in Children and Adolescents" (*Pediatric Clinics of North America*, October 1990), was written by Dr. David Webb at the Center for Sports Medicine, Saint Francis Memorial Hospital, San Francisco, California. He found that most injuries occurred in the home and were unsupervised and that there is not an inordinate risk of injury in weight training if it's properly done. He also reported that strength training can help kids excel in sports and that it can actually reduce the incidence of muscle or tendon injuries in sports.

A February 2, 2006 note from the Mayo Clinic on their Web page, www.mayoclinic.com, said: "Strength training for kids has gotten a bad reputation over the years. Lifting weights, for example, was once thought to damage young growth plates—areas of cartilage that have not yet turned to bone. Experts now realize that with good technique and the right amount of resistance, young athletes can avoid growth plate injuries. Strengthening exercises, with proper training and supervision, provide many benefits to a young athlete."

What does this all mean? Knowledgeable trainers can help young athletes gain strength at all levels of play, and weight training will help them do so. Since most kids are urged to do it, those who don't will be at a disadvantage. However, any program should avoid maximal weight lifts until the mid-high-school years.

Be careful; injury can still occur no matter how careful you are. Let's face it: Anyone who has ever lifted weights knows that, even if you follow a good program, kids have a powerful urge to finish up with some heavy weights to see how much they can lift. If unsupervised, they will go for the max at some point. This is one of the main reasons I frown on the idea. I also resent the idea that we should heighten the competitive pressure of athletics in grade school by creating a need to strength train to "keep up." However, the reality is that, at the high-school level, players will need to lift weights if they are to be competitive. As a parent, you must ensure that they are supervised and that they follow a sound program. A 7 percent injury rate for unsupervised training is quite high, so parents must assert controls on this matter.

A player who undertakes a strength-training program, as advised above, should have the supervision and advice of a knowledgeable trainer. Parents should ask their doctor if any preexisting health conditions can be aggravated by such training. High blood pressure is one condition that doesn't mix with weights. Any pain should be reported to the trainer. Warm-up and stretching exercises should be done before lifting. Lifting maximal weights or engaging in ballistic, sudden, jerking exercises such as clean and jerk should not be allowed. Kids should generally use weights that can be done in sets of fifteen repetitions. They should not lift every day, but every other day at the most. All major muscle groups should get some attention to keep development balanced.

In the weight room, basketball players should emphasize legs (upper and lower) and upper body (shoulders, arms, and wrists). I already mentioned partial squats. Do hamstring curls, too. A good calf exercise is to sit on a chair with weight on the top of the thighs and toes on a block of wood. Raise the weight by pushing the toes against the block and raising the heels. Exercises with dumbbells for shoulder, wrist, and forearm are great, especially for rebounding. Bench presses will help—it's better if the bench inclines. Do wrist curls also. Let the trainer explain how to do these and other exercises needed for a balanced program.

PLYOMETRICS: INCREASE VERTICAL LEAPING

Plyometrics is a method of developing power by rapidly stretching and contracting specific muscles under significant resistance. When performed in rapid succession, this stretching and contracting cycle allows the muscles to store some of the energy lost in the stretching phase for use during the contraction phase. Plyometrics is currently viewed as one of the best ways, if not the best way, to improve power, and it is a growing practice, not only in power sports such as football, but has been used to increase power in other areas. One such area is in developing leaping ability for basketball. Power is similar to strength, except you are adding a time factor; that is, a person will leap higher if they have more power in that moment of contraction, more speed in the contraction itself. So what we are looking at is not just the contraction of the muscle, but how fast it will contract.

We know that a muscle will contract the fastest when it has been *loaded* or stretched first. A basketball player jumps higher, as we all know, if she crouches down a bit just before the jump, thus loading or stretching the thigh muscles, and then contracting, pushing upward.

Plyometrics is the way we practice how to perform a power movement better, by shortening the time it takes for the muscles to contract, resulting in more power.

Having said all of this, I don't support use of such power training at beginner or intermediate levels, and coaches should probably just avoid it altogether. At advanced levels, competition is such that players need to keep up with others, find a way to get an edge, and so plyometric training is unavoidable. At young ages, before fifteen, joints are still forming. Jumping form is not well developed, and powerful thrusts can lead to injury. If a kid can't squat twice his body weight, I'd stay away from it. Plus, it's just not that

174

important. The following, however, are some plyometric drills, the first two of which do not yield a great stress on joints. The third should be reserved for advanced levels. Players should be warmed up before trying these drills. There are an infinite number of plyometric exercises to increase vertical leap, but here are a few good ones commonly used.

Two-foot Ankle Hop (Beginner Level). Players keep their feet together and, remaining in one place, hop up and down using only their ankles and calves. Have the players concentrate on getting as high as possible and exploding off the floor as soon as they can after landing.

Rapid Jumps (Intermediate Level). Players stand under a hoop or another object which is reachable. Have the players jump up, touching the object; alternate hands each time. Players should focus on jumping as high as possible, then exploding back up very quickly after landing.

Box Jumps (Advanced). This is the classic plyometric exercise. Place two one- to two-feet-high boxes that will support a player's weight about two to three feet from each other. Players stand on the top of the box and step out. They drop to the floor and immediately jump back up to the other box. Make sure the boxes will not move or slide; such boxes are sold in sporting goods stores. Have the players repeat several times. Difficulty increases with the height of the boxes. Jumping onto a soft surface such as a mat is preferable at first.

VISION

The following will be the most important section in this book for some of your players, maybe for your own child. It reveals what may be the best-kept secret in basketball and perhaps in all of sports. It's about vision and eyesight: how critical it is and how to improve it. Much research has been done, and many studies estimate that vision problems affect 20 to 25 percent of school-aged children. Vision disorders have been considered one of the most prevalent handicapping conditions in childhood.

Check your child and be alert to symptoms in your players. They include: rubbing the eyes, eyestrain or headaches after reading, difficulty concentrating while reading, words seeming to move on the page, reading too close to the eyes, confusing left and right, squinting, blinking a lot, losing place while reading, short attention span. If you see any of these symptoms, especially if a few are present, think about getting an eye test.

As I look back on my nearly three decades of coaching sports, I'm reminded of the many young players who came to the game full of hope and excitement but who just never made it. Surely, for many, it just wasn't there. Their gifts of life were elsewhere, in the laboratory, with music, or in other skills, just not in basketball. That's life. But I have become convinced that, for many, a substantial part of the problem was merely in their inability to see clearly enough to shoot with precision, catch a short quick pass, or see the whole floor of play.

I'm not describing major differences in eyesight in this chapter. Just a small subtle difference in visual acuity is enough to lead to significant differences in how well one can catch, pass, dribble, or shoot basketballs.

This fact is not lost on professional players. Vision therapy is a rapidly growing staple of the off-season preparation of players in most professional sports. The sports literature reports that most other sports such as golf, tennis, hockey, and baseball are including emphasis on visual acuity in training routines. This eye training consists of a series of vision tests, exercises for the fourteen eye muscles, and follow-up workouts designed to improve concentration, visual focus, depth perception, and hand-eye coordination.

The good news is that vision can be improved. Even if your child has 20/20 vision, this does not mean he cannot improve other aspects of vision, such as depth perception, the ability to clearly track a fast-moving object, and hand-eye coordination. The difference, with only a small amount of therapy, can be enormous. In 2005, the American Optometric Association said "there is sufficient scientific support for the efficacy of vision therapy in modifying and improving oculomotor, accommodative, and binocular system disorders, as measured by standardized clinical and laboratory testing methods, in the majority of patients of all ages for whom it is properly undertaken and employed."

It is not the objective of this book to give medical advice or to go into depth on the biology of the eye itself. I advise you to see an eye doctor to have your child's eyes tested. If one of your players seems to have some difficulty seeing the ball, suggest an exam to the parents. Tell them to read this book, so they can consider whether it would be useful to engage in vision therapy, even if there is a more obvious eye disorder.

Vision therapy has advanced far enough that some exercises can safely be done at home. I'll list a few that appear more commonly in the literature and that apply to the skills needed in basketball. Again, the best practice is to first seek a doctor's advice.

VISION THERAPY DRILLS

Brock String Drill. Tie a four-foot string, with a large knot or black tape marking the center and a mark several inches from each end, to an object at your child's sitting eye level. Have the player stretch the line taut and hold it against her nose. When she looks

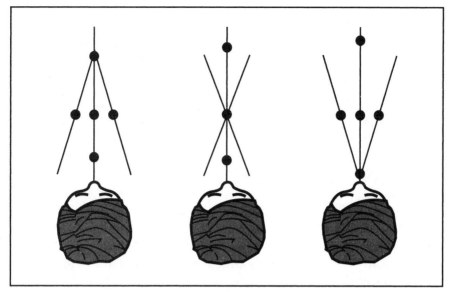

The Brock string-vision therapy drill improves focusing and depth perception. See the text for a detailed explanation of the drill.

at the center spot, she will see an X pattern. (See figure 10-1.) When she looks at the far spot, she'll see an A pattern, and, at the near spot, a V pattern. Have her practice shifting the gaze from spot to spot until it feels smooth and easy to do. Eventually you can shorten the string. Have the player do this exercise for several minutes each day. It will improve her focusing and depth perception. This drill can be done at home or at practice. (Check with parents first!)

Marsden Ball Drill. Get a rubber ball about four inches in diameter. Suspend it from overhead to the player's sitting eye level. Write letters and numbers all over the ball in ink. (They should be clear, dark letters on a light-colored ball.) Have the player cover one eye and tap the ball lightly. He should try to call out a letter he sees and quickly touch it with his finger. Have the player do this exercise with each eye for a few minutes. This improves eye-hand coordination and the ability to track a moving object. The player should try to maintain a fluid and continuous pace. He can use a smaller ball to make it tougher. With parental consent, the Marsden ball drill can be done at practice. Have one player hold the string for another.

Fixation Drill. Hang a ring from a string at standing eye level. Have the player stand a step away with a long pencil. The player covers the left eye, steps toward the ring with the right foot, and, holding the pencil in the right hand, tries to put the pencil through the ring without touching it. After a few minutes, he switches eyes, steps with the left foot, and uses the left hand. After a player has mastered this drill, have him try it with a moving target. This drill improves hand-eye coordination.

Rotations Drill. Place a marble in a pie tin or frying pan held about fifteen to eighteen inches from the player's eyes. The player holds her head still, rotates the marble, and tries to follow it for a few minutes. Have the player change direction for another two minutes. This improves tracking ability.

Accommodation Drill. Doctors use a device called an Accomotrac, based on biofeedback theory, to improve focusing problems, particularly nearsightedness. An exercise a player can do is to sit with a newspaper with normal-sized print at just below eye level, as close as possible to the eye, then place another newspaper with large headlines fifteen to twenty feet away. The player covers one eye, then shifts his focus back and forth from one newspaper to the other. This can be done with any nearby small object and any distant object.

Convergence Drill. Place this book on a desk with figure 10-2 at normal reading distance. Have the player hold a pencil between the two sets of circles and slowly move the pencil point toward his eyes. At a point about six inches from his eyes, a third circle

10–2. **CONVERGENCE CIRCLES**

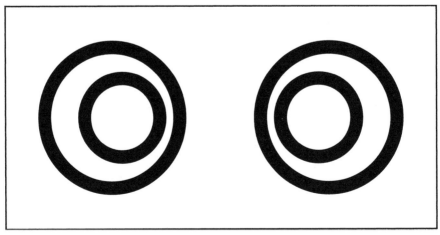

Use these circles when practicing the convergence drill.

will appear between the other two. The outer circle should appear closer than the inner one. When it seems clear, the player shifts his eyes to something else and brings them back again to the pencil tip. Have the player do this until his focus remains smooth and clear upon the middle figure. The player repeats this exercise ten times.

Another convergence drill is for the player to hold the circles up at reading distance, but just below eye level. The player sits several feet from a wall, then focuses on the wall, and the third circle should again appear. This time, the small inner circle should appear closer. The player closes his eyes and reopens them to the pencil point. Have the player do this several times until his focus stays smooth and clear. After this is mastered, the pencil can be dispensed with, and the distance of the figures can be made a bit closer. You can also draw the figures on separate cards and separate them more (just a bit, don't let the player strain). He should always try to get to a clear focus on the center set of circles.

Teach these drills to your players at a practice. Tell them to do them at home. Some can be done on the court by subs, during scrimmages, or just before practice. Talk to parents first. Tell parents to get this book and read this section. Your team's vision will improve. Shooting, passing, and receiving will improve. Hopefully, some of those kids who otherwise wouldn't make it will have some fun with this great game!

One final thought. Do you know which of your eyes is dominant? Make a circle with your thumb and index finger, and extend your arm out at eye level. Fix your sight on a small object and close one eye, then open it and close the other. The dominant eye is the one for which the object does not move! Shooters should turn their heads a bit so the dominant eye looks more directly at the hoop.

INJURIES

Is there a trainer or someone qualified in first aid at practice? This is very important during the early days of practice. Most leagues require coaches to obtain licenses that expose them to first-aid techniques, but is there someone who really knows what to do? If not, remember that parents can take a course and become quite knowledgeable. Perhaps you can get a parent to volunteer as a trainer.

I watched a practice game once in which a kid twisted a knee. The coach was short-handed for players and seemed more concerned about getting the kid back into the game than worried about the extent of any injury. A few minutes later, the kid was back in the action. After a while, I noticed he was limping a bit. The coach never looked at him. I told the coach, and the player was removed. As a parent, it pays to attend a few practices to see how sensitive the coach is to injury. A good rule is that a player who complains of any injury to any joint cannot play for at least ten minutes to see if pain or swelling is present.

No matter how well-conditioned a team is, injuries can occur anytime. A common injury is a groin strain, usually caused by sprinting down the court without warming up. Blisters, nosebleeds, finger jams, floor burns, muscle cramps, shin splints, and athlete's foot are the most common basketball injuries. Shin splints are a painful soreness in the shins which arises from play on different surfaces (indoor and outdoor) or from not warming up. Make sure your players wear socks covering the shins to keep them warm. Athlete's foot is a fungus that thrives in damp, warm environments. There are good antiseptic powers for this. Players should thoroughly dry their feet after practice and change socks frequently. Sprained or strained wrists and forearms, as well as sprained ankles and bruises, also occur fairly frequently. Thankfully, broken bones are rare, but not rare enough. Most youth basketball teams don't have trained first-aid people, and they should. I went through the program for my son's team, and it was quite good.

Abrasions, or floor burns, often occur on the sides of the legs and elbows, from sliding on the gym floor. These are the most likely cuts to get infected. Wash the wound as soon as possible, with soap if it is handy. Apply a dressing when you can—the sooner the better. Just put some antiseptic on it. If it gets red or pussy, or red tracks appear, have the player see a physician.

Lacerations are deeper wounds. Unless bleeding is severe, wash the wound and apply direct pressure with a bandage (you can tie the knot right over the wound to reinforce the pressure). Immediately elevate the wound higher than the heart to help slow the bleeding. If the bandage over the wound gets blood-soaked, don't remove it—just apply a new dressing right over it. If the child has lost a lot of blood, you'll need to treat for shock. Keep the player warm with blankets, and call for help. If a laceration is major, a butterfly bandage will hold the skin together. Consult a physician immediately for stitches.

Contusions and bruises occur frequently. Apply ice quickly after taking care of any abrasions or lacerations. Ice arrests internal bleeding and prevents or lessens swelling. Ice is the best first-aid available for nearly any swelling from bruises or sprains. Apply it very quickly, within minutes, and much internal damage will be spared. Do not move the child, especially if he is down due to a hard collision. He could have a spinal injury, and the slightest movement by an untrained person could do some serious damage.

Sprained ankles, knees, or wrists should be immobilized. Apply an ice pack immediately. Act as if there is a fracture until you're sure there is none. Call the ambulance if there is any question in your mind. Get an x-ray to see if there is a break or other damage.

If there is a fracture, immobilize the child completely when possible. There should be no movement at all. Comfort her, get her warm with coats or blankets, and get medical help. Do not allow the child to be moved or cared for by anyone who is not medically trained. If she is in the middle of the court during a championship game, the game can wait! Insist on this. Permanent damage can result from aggravating a break.

If a child ever falls to the ground unconscious, see if anyone present has been trained in first aid. The first move, once it is clear that the child will not respond, is to check for the vital signs—airway, breathing, and circulation—the ABCs of first aid. Send for an ambulance and let a trained person administer rescue breathing or CPR (cardiopulmonary resuscitation) as necessary. Try to stay calm and let the first-aiders do their job. In all my years of coaching four sports, and playing even more, I've never seen CPR needed. I hope that you won't either.

Finally, heat exhaustion can occur during practices or games, particularly late in the game. The body gets clammy and pale. Remove the child from the game, apply cool towels, and elevate his feet. If the body temperature is very high and his pupils are constricted, you should suspect heat stroke. Call an ambulance and cool him down fast. Treat for shock.

Knee injuries are tough. Often the injury will require some sort of arthroscopic surgery to mend cartilage. Modern procedures are quite advanced and simple. Have the child see a knowledgeable sports doctor.

Tell your child to play the game safely. Aggressiveness is okay, but players should never intentionally hurt someone. Hope that other parents do the same. I play various sports frequently, and there are often one or two guys who take chances with the health of others. Don't encourage your child to grow up to be like them.

When an injury occurs, insist on rest. I've seen many kids rush back from a sprained ankle only to have the injury plague them through the years. Don't let this happen. And make sure that the child wears an ankle brace from then on. There are excellent ankle braces on the market today. Get one. The point is that injuries need time to heal right. If you give them that time, the future can have many years of sports for your child. If you don't, it could be over already.

SERIOUS INJURIES

Catastrophic spine or brain injuries among any athletes, especially basketball players, are rare, yet they happen. There are cases, for example, where a kid hits a wall or obstruction with her head. This is obviously a most unpleasant subject, but it is important that you understand some detail. Many deadly injuries of the brain or paralyzing injuries of the spine are caused by an earlier blow, sometimes one that occurred a week or more earlier, and a concerned and informed parent can step in and avoid it. A player can receive a concussion, never black out, and the brain swelling can then become lethal days later, if triggered by a relatively minor blow.

The point is that any level of confusion or headache brought on by a blow to the head should receive immediate medical attention. I don't care if it's a championship game—get the player out of the game! The Colorado Medical Society recommends that a player who sustains a severe blow to the head be removed from a game for at least twenty minutes and not be allowed to return to the game if any confusion or amnesia persists during that time. A player who loses consciousness should go straight to the hospital.

THE CARBOHYDRATE DIET

Parents can do only so much to improve their child's athletic ability, but they can do a great deal to maintain his or her good health. All sports require a great deal of energy, and a healthy body goes a long way toward performing better on the court and avoiding injury.

Obviously, a balanced diet is essential. There are many books on diet, and your doctor or school nurse can also advise on the elements of good diet. Good nutrition helps develop strength, endurance, and concentration. A good diet balances proteins, carbohydrates, and fats. An athlete in training needs mainly complex carbohydrates, about 70 percent of the total diet, with fats (10 percent) and proteins (20 percent) splitting the remainder. Popular today is the Food Guide Pyramid. Complex carbohydrates dominate the base grouping, reflecting the greater doses of breads, cereal, rice, and pasta that are recommended. Vegetables and fruits take up the next level, calling for a few daily servings each. The dairy group and the meat, fish, and poultry group are next, with fats last.

Early in the season, an evening meal high in carbohydrates helps maintain energy the next day. Pasta is the best meal for this. A banana each day during this early period helps prevent potassium depletion. Potassium facilitates the process of muscular contraction. Complex carbohydrates are the primary source of fuel and energy for the athlete. What the body doesn't need, it stores for future use. Players should avoid simple carbohydrates such as sugar and honey. The adage that a candy bar just before a game gives an energy boost is misleading, since simple carbohydrates cause unstable supplies of glucose. (Ever notice how tired you feel after a sweets overload?) Good sources of complex carbohydrates are corn on the cob, wild rice, brown rice, whole wheat, and whole rye.

Because children have special fluid needs, fluids play a critical role in maintaining the health and performance of the child athlete. Heat stroke ranks second among reported causes of death in high-school athletes. Most teams allow water breaks, so make sure parents know to get their child a water bottle. Mid-practice is not a good time to load up on water, so tell the kids to limit themselves to a cup at each break. Kids need a couple of quarts a day, more if it's hot and they are playing outside. Drinking plenty of water is a good habit, so be sure they know to drink some at each meal. It is also important to drink plenty of fluids before, during, and after practices. Dehydration reduces performance and can lead to serious medical problems.

Sufficient sleep is also a concern. If your son or daughter starts the season with hard sessions of practice, you won't have to worry too much at first, since your child will come right home and hit the pillow. However, into the season, particularly at high-school levels, a player may try to burn the candle at both ends. Again, I find that kids relate better when they consider practical consequences of their actions. Lack of sufficient rest diminishes performance. Diminished performance costs playing time.

EATING DISORDERS

This book is not a medical treatise, and you should consult a physician on any medical issue. But coaches and parents must be aware of eating disorders and how they affect the athletes. There are two such eating disorders, and they often (about half the time) are found together. Anorexia Nervosa is a fear of gaining weight, leading one to diet in an extreme and unhealthy manner. The second, Bulimia, is forced purging, often after a period of binge eating. The binges and purges are often planned and quite secretive. Onset of eating disorders is most prevalent from 15-20 years of age and usually occures in girls.

As a coach or parent, you need to be aware and on the lookout for eating disorders. It may be difficult because many kids are thin but seem quite healthy. Moreover, often parents miss or are in denial about a problem, saying "Oh, she is just nice and thin." But I always felt as a coach that I had an independent responsibility to players. Obviously, the first step is to talk about it with the player and her parents, but you have the right to call for a physical if you are concerned about a child's health. In fact, I would argue it is your duty to do so. If a player is sick, the rigors of athletic competition will contribute to the health problem.

SPECIAL CONSIDERATIONS FOR GIRLS

A girl's menstrual cycle most commonly begins at about eleven to twelve years old, and, in some cases, by age nine. The first menstrual period of an adolescent girl is known as the menarche. Studies have proven that intense exercise can delay the onset of menarche, by disrupting the hormonal patterns that control menstruation. A girl who has not reached menarche by age fifteen would be considered abnormal by most doctors.

For some women, menstrual cycles are painful, so limited activity during their cycle is their norm. However, the menstrual cycle does not compromise performance. In fact, about one-third of all female Olympic gold medals were won during menstruation. Two-thirds were gained a week after the cessation of the period.

In 1996, the Surgeon General detailed the significant and overriding benefits of exercise and sports for both sexes. However, research still shows that exercise can result in menstrual dysfunction for some women. As noted above, amenorrhea is not uncommon among women athletes, and it is one of the triad of problems. It is closely related to poor nutrition and rigorous training. However, it's not likely to appear until later in high school.

The nutrition needs of women, related to menstruation, are significant and worthy of special mention here. Poor nutrition in female athletes often reveals itself in the form of tiredness, uneven performance, injuries, or burnout. The player's diet should consist of about 70 percent carbohydrates and 20 percent protein. The daily requirement of iron for girls is 18 mg. Excessive sweating and menstruation can further exacerbate iron loss. Iron-rich foods, dietary supplements, and vitamin C (which helps absorb iron) can improve performance. Caffeine intake blocks iron uptake. Calcium intake is another nutrient for which female athletes have higher needs, but fall far short of the mark. Stress fractures, which can sideline a girl for the remainder of a season, are the most tangible risk. Weight-bearing sports, those that involve running or jumping like basketball, carry the greatest risk.

COACHES' AND PARENTS' CHECKLIST

11

Now it's time to get out to the basketball court with your child or team. When I coach, I find it useful to have a checklist of things to look for or to say as I work with my kids. The checklist below is a reminder. Repetition of key phrases helps your child concentrate on basics.

DRIBBLING: TOP TEN FUNDAMENTALS

The best confidence builder for a beginner.

- ☐ Keep the ball out on the fingers.
- ☐ Receive the ball, withdraw the hand, cradle it, and pump back out.
- ☐ Arm and body move with the rhythm of the ball.
- ☐ Develop both hands.
- ☐ Head up, eyes front.
- ☐ Keep ball and body low in traffic.
- ☐ Shield ball with body.
- ☐ Use the pivot freely.
- ☐ Feint and change speeds.
- ☐ Don't pick up the dribble.

PASSING: TOP TEN FUNDAMENTALS

- ☐ Use two hands.
- ☐ Spread fingers in W shape.
- ☐ Rotate fingertips up under chin and into chest area.
- ☐ Step toward the receiver.
- ☐ Pass to the receiver's chest or outstretched hand.
- ☐ Quick, snappy passes are critical to good team play.

☐ Lead the receiver. Pass to open space.

☐ Don't broadcast the pass.

☐ Pass to the side of receiver opposite the defender.

☐ React. Know what's happening!

RECEIVING PASSES: TOP FIVE FUNDAMENTALS

☐ Always know where the ball is and want/expect it.

☐ Move to the pass.

☐ Give a target hand.

☐ Soft hands.

☐ Keep the eyes on the ball.

SHOOTING: TOP TEN FUNDAMENTALS

The essence of basketball.

☐ Shoot with relaxed confidence within your range.

☐ Triple-threat balance.

☐ Fakes make space: Jab step to get free.

☐ Jump high and straight, off both feet.

☐ Cradle high.

☐ Point elbow and foot to hoop, power comes from the lower body.

☐ Soft robotic release, flick wrist, 30-degree reverse spin, gooseneck finish.

☐ Aim to sit ball on point of hoop closest to you.

☐ Achieve reasonable arc.

☐ Follow the shot.

LAY-UPS: TOP SIX FUNDAMENTALS

☐ Claim the lane.

☐ Stay low.

☐ Take two big steps when ready to jump.

☐ Lift knee on shooting-hand side.

☐ Lay ball up softly.

☐ Rotate landing.

FREE THROWS: TOP EIGHT FUNDAMENTALS

☐ Practice constantly.

☐ Center shooting-side foot on foul line and point it at the hoop.

☐ Be comfortable.

☐ Start low.

☐ Cradle, raise high, flick, and gooseneck.

☐ Point elbow at hoop.

☐ Square head and shoulders.

☐ Extend body fully, up on toes, and hold extension.

OFFENSE: TOP TEN CONCEPTS

☐ Know the offensive zones. Run the offense.

☐ Look for high-percentage shot, in shooter's range, without undue defensive pressure.

☐ Attack from wing.

☐ Penetrate to the post underneath.

☐ Screen, screen, and more screen.

☐ Create motion: Give and go.

☐ Don't be too quick to dribble.

☐ Pass to open space.

☐ Move off the ball.

☐ Follow the shot.

DEFENSE: TOP TEN CONCEPTS

☐ Transition: Get back on defense quickly.

☐ Triple-threat form.

☐ Threaten, dog, trap, smother: Confuse the ballhandler.

☐ Force the ball wide, away from the lane.

☐ Avoid bad fouls, especially underneath.

☐ Deny a pass by fronting players underneath.

☐ Fight through or sink behind screen.

☐ Resist the fake

☐ Ball-You-Player. Defend your opponent from the ball side and look for steals, track ball with ball-side hand.

☐ Box out, rebound, catch with two hands.

11

GLOSSARY

Airball: An outside shot that misses the hoop, backboard, everything. At high school and college games, fans will razz a player who has shot an airball every time he gets his hands on the ball thereafter.

Alley-Oop Pass: A high pass thrown over the defense to a player near the basket.

Arc: The path of a shot ball. A low arc is called a brick; an overly high arc is a rainmaker. Ordinarily, an arc should be about fifteen feet from the floor on a fifteen-foot jump shot.

Backboard: The rectangular or semicircular fan-shaped surface on which the basket is mounted, used for bank shots. It is also called the glass, if so constructed. In outside lots, it's usually made of wood or metal. The backboard can be called a bankboard or a bangboard.

Backcourt: The half of the court where the ball isn't in play. In the early days, some players stayed back on defense all the time, by rule, and were called backcourt players. Now the team is used to describe the area itself, and the offense can't take the ball into the backcourt area once they completely cross the mid-court line (also called the backcourt line).

Backdoor Cut: An off-the-ball move by an offensive player along the baseline, slipping "underneath" the defense, looking for a pass.

Bank Shot: The ball hits the backboard before it goes through the basket. Sometimes it's just a lucky shot, although the shooter will smile as though he intended to bank it.

Baseline: The end-line boundary at each end of the court, under the hoop. A baseline drive is very effective if the player can get by the defender. The baseline, however, is out-of-bounds.

Basket: The eighteen-inch circumference hoop that players shoot at. Also known as a bucket. When the ball goes through, it is a field goal, and one, two, or three points are awarded.

Block: To reject or repel a shot ball before it hits the top of its arc.

Box-out: A defensive move using the back of the body to screen a player from getting a rebound.

Bury: To make a shot cleanly. Not touching the rim.

Center: Usually the tallest player on the team. The center plays underneath, in the lane, where the action is.

Charge: An offensive or player-control foul committed by a driving offensive player hitting a stationary defender who has established his position. The defense gets possession.

Circle: An offensive move without the ball, in which the player circles his defender to turn and confuse him and then breaks free for a pass.

Crash: Running toward the hoop after a shot is taken to get a rebound, called "crashing the boards."

Cut: A move without the ball. The player dashes into or across the lane, looking for a pass.

Defense: The endeavor to get possession of the ball and prevent the opposition from scoring points.

Deny: The endeavor to prevent a player being open for a pass by blocking the passing lane with the body or at least an arm.

Double-team: Two on one defense, usually in the corners.

Downtown: A shot far from the hoop, well beyond the three-point line.

Dribble: To advance the ball by bouncing it with either hand. The feet can do no more than a pivot move if the player has the ball but is not dribbling. Once the dribble is stopped, it can't start again, or a double-dribble violation is called. Dribbles can be behind the back or between the legs to keep the ball away from a defender.

Drive: A running dribble toward the hoop for a shot up close.

Dunk: A shot in which the player places the ball directly into the hoop, also called a slam, stuff, jam. If the player spins 180 degrees, it's a reverse slam.

Fake: The art of getting a defender off balance or moving in one direction so the offensive player can move in another. The player usually moves the head or the ball, or even takes a step in one direction and then suddenly goes in another. A player can also fake a shot, called a pump fake, to get the defender to jump, and then the shooter goes up as the defender comes down. Players can put a series of fakes together to get a defender off balance.

Fast break: Moving the ball upcourt quickly, by virtue of a long pass to a player running upcourt. The defense never gets set. The team doing the fast break uses their speed and needs endurance.

Flash: Quick movements from one side of the free-throw lane to the other, usually by a big player posting up at one side, then flashing across the lane to the other.

Follow-up: Moving to the boards after taking a shot. Usually a player fades to the opposite side of the court from the shot, since most rebounds bounce to the opposite side.

Forward: In the early days, the forward was an offensive player who was allowed to move across the mid-court line and play offense. Now, the term refers to a tall player who takes a position near the baseline on either side of the hoop.

Foul: Illegal contact between two players with any part of the body. The player causing the contact gets the foul; the other team gets possession or a shot, depending on the type of foul. A personal foul is contact with an opponent. A common foul is a personal foul which is neither flagrant, intentional, nor committed against a player trying for a field goal. An intentional foul is violent or savage. A technical foul is a non-contact foul. A player-control foul, also known as a charge, is committed by a ballhandler.

Foul out: Once a player has accumulated five personal fouls, he is disqualified from the game. The limit is six fouls in the pros.

Free throw: A free shot awarded to a player who is fouled. The shot is taken from the free-throw line, fifteen feet from the hoop.

Free-throw lane: The twelve-foot-wide area bounded by the free-throw lines, also called the paint, inside the lane, or underneath. This area is where most of the action occurs in basketball.

Freeze: A type of offense which patiently, slowly controls the ball, either to waste time on the clock or to wait for a high-percentage shot.

Front: Similar to "deny." The player blocks the passing lane with his body to deny a pass, usually to a big player. Unlike denying, which can occur anywhere, fronting always occurs underneath.

Give and go: A pass to a teammate, a dash toward the hoop past the defender, and a return pass for the lay-up. The bread-and-butter play of basketball.

Gooseneck: The position of the hand and forearm after a shot, resembling a goose's neck.

Guard: The name given to the players who bring the ball upcourt. They used to be defensive players only, guarding the defensive area, not allowed past mid-court. The point guard is the play-maker, a ballhandler. The off guard is a shooting guard.

Inbounds: The playing area. A ball is passed from out-of-bounds after a field goal (a basket) or any time the ball goes out of bounds. A player has only five seconds to inbound and must start from the spot designated by the referee, except after a field goal.

Incidental Contact: Minor or inadvertent contact with an opponent, ignored by the official.

Jab: A fake pivot step toward a defender to drive her back and get some room for a shot or pass. A reverse jab does the opposite, with the player heading away from the basket and then breaking toward it. Also called a rocker step.

Jump ball: The opening play of the game. Two players meet at mid-court, and the referee throws the ball up between them. They must tap it to teammates who are waiting outside the large mid-court circle. Jump balls used to occur whenever two opposing players were in equal possession of the ball, but now, even though such situations are called "jump balls," the ball is just awarded alternatively to either team depending on which direction the possession arrow is facing (to speed up the game).

Jump shots: See Shots.

Jump stop: When a moving player comes to catch a pass or a rebound, jumping onto both feet on the balls of the toes, so that either foot can then be the pivot foot. It sets up the balanced triple-threat position.

Key: The term used to designate the area including the free-throw lane and the free-throw circle. The top of the key, the point of the circle farthest from the hoop, is the area where most plays are initiated.

Lay-up: See Shots.

Lob: A high pass over a defender, usually a fast-break pass to a streaking guard or a pass over a defender fronting a player underneath.

Man-to-Man: One-on-one defense, guarding a specific player instead of an area.

Offense: The endeavor to score points by making field goals. A motion offense uses speed, screens, and shooting ability; a power offense looks for the big players underneath.

Officials: The referees. They make sure the game is played by the rules. Basketball officials are the most harassed people in all sports. The game is fast, and the fans are very close. This leads to much disagreement. The official referee signals of the National Federation of State High School Associations are reproduced in on pages 193–195.

Outlet: A wing player, near the sideline, who sets up for a pass from a defensive rebounder. The idea is for the player to set up away from any defenders so the rebounder can get the ball quickly out from underneath.

Overshift: Defending off center, to the strong side of a player. If a player is right-handed, the defender shifts a bit to that side, placing the left foot forward and blocking that lane.

Palming: A player dribbling the ball may not lift the ball nor change its direction from underneath with the palm. This is also called "carrying." Through the 1990s, referees tended to ignore these violations unless flagrant, but have since been calling the violation more often.

Perimeter: The outside edge of the normal shooting distance—normally about seventeen to nineteen feet from the hoop.

Period: In youth ball, a game is divided into four periods, or quarters, of six to eight minutes each, depending on the level of play. In the pros, these periods are twelve minutes each. In college, however, there are two twenty-minute halves.

Pick: Screening a defender who is guarding a player with the ball so he can dribble around the defender.

Pivot: A move performed when a player is in possession of the ball, but not dribbling, stepping and stretching in any direction with one foot, while the toes of the other foot are in continuous contact with the floor. The pivot foot can spin but not lift or slide without causing a traveling violation.

Plyometrics: The strength conditioning of muscles by stretching and contracting them under sudden, strong pressure.

Point: The area at the top of the key from which most plays commence.

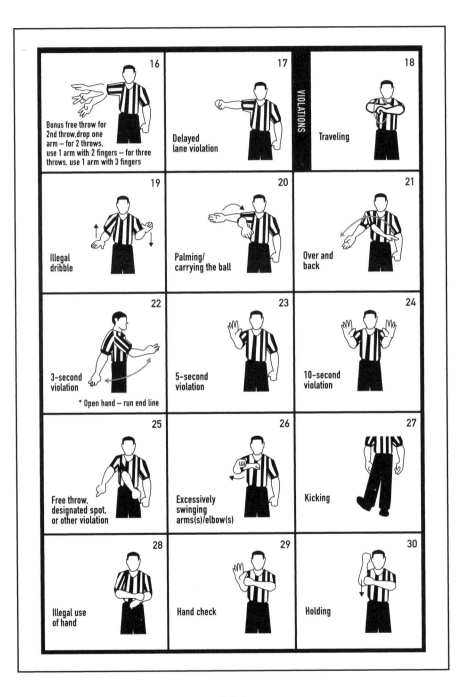

16 Bonus free throw for 2nd throw, drop one arm — for 2 throws, use 1 arm with 2 fingers — for three throws, use 1 arm with 3 fingers	**17** Delayed lane violation	VIOLATIONS **18** Traveling
19 Illegal dribble	**20** Palming/ carrying the ball	**21** Over and back
22 3-second violation * Open hand — run end line	**23** 5-second violation	**24** 10-second violation
25 Free throw, designated spot, or other violation	**26** Excessively swinging arms(s)/elbow(s)	**27** Kicking
28 Illegal use of hand	**29** Hand check	**30** Holding

194

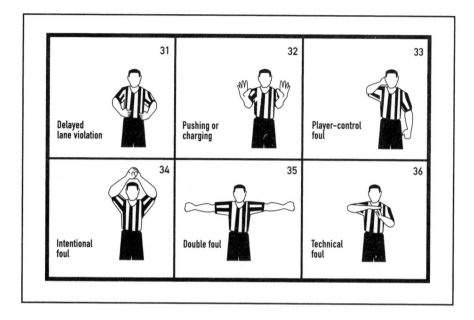

Possession Arrow: When a jump ball is called during a game, the referee looks to the possession arrow on the scorer's table to see which team's turn it is to get possession. The arrow is then reset to point the other way, signaling that the next jump ball is awarded to the other team.

Post: The area underneath the basket. This term also describes a move by which a big player screens his defender with his back while awaiting a pass and then rolls to either side to score. See chapter one.

Press: Full-court defense. This is an endeavor to harass and frustrate the players bringing the ball upcourt. The hope is that the pressure will force a mistake leading to a turnover.

Quarter: See Period.

Rebound: A missed shot which bounces off the rim or backboard onto the field of play. The attempt to secure this loose ball is called rebounding.

Scissor: A play in which two offensive players crisscross in front of a third player, usually at a high post.

Screen: Gaining a set position in a lane and preventing a defender from moving, thus freeing the player defended. Used interchangeably with the term "pick," although screen often refers to a play off the ball.

Scrimmage: A practice game, usually intra-squad.

Shin splints: A common ailment involving pain in the shin area, sometimes quite painful. They often occur from playing on harder surfaces or before a player is properly conditioned. Socks should always be worn at full height to keep this area warm.

Shots: There are many. The lay-up and jump shot are the dominant shots. Set shots are jump shots without a jump, usually from a far, undefended distance. A foul shot is a set shot. Underneath, there are hook shots and dunks. Short jump shots often use the backboard in a bank shot. Three-point shots are from about nineteen feet, nine inches or farther. A fade-away shot is a fading backward jump shot. Some shots get their name from the floor position from which the shot is taken (e.g., corner, top of the key, half-court, high post). A double-pump is a fake shot followed by a shot off a lay-up. Names of shots also vary a bit by region. But the bread-and-butter are the lay-ups and jumpers, and that's where the kids should start.

Shuffle: A motion or continuity pattern offensive play, whereby all players continuously move according to a set pattern, looking for opportunities to score.

Soft touch: A term used to identify short shots which softly hit the rim and drop in. They usually flow from good form, good ball control, and hand coordination. Players who consistently shoot in such a manner are said to have a "soft touch."

Square: Setting the shoulders perpendicular or slightly at angles to the hoop before shooting. The main idea is one of balance and being set.

Stall: This is an attempt to waste time, often near the end of a game, by passing around the perimeter. Some teams use it to slow down the tempo or keep the score close against a better team. It used to be allowed forever, so the shot clock was instituted at some levels to require a team to shoot in a designated amount of seconds, although there is no shot clock in youth basketball.

Strong side: Often, especially against a zone defense, the offense will place an extra man to one side. This also happens naturally on the side the ball is on.

Superman: A drill for shooting or rebounding consecutively and alternately from each side of the basket, back and forth.

Switch: A defensive move in which two offensive players crisscross or pick and roll; they switch and guard each other's man.

Technical Foul: A foul called for a procedural violation or misconduct, usually unsportsmanlike conduct, resulting in a free throw and possession awarded to the other team. Two such fouls will result in ejection from the game.

Three-Point Line: Actually introduced by the now defunct American Basketball League in 1961 to increase scoring. The three-point line in high-school and college ball is nineteen feet, nine inches from the basket, and a shot from entirely beyond that line scores three points. In the pros, it's from twenty-three feet, nine inches.

Three-second violation: This violation occurs when an offensive player has at least part of a foot in the lane for more than three seconds.

Tip: To tap the ball to another player or toward the hoop without catching it. Used often to steal passes or tap rebounds.

Trailer: A player who follows a driving ball-handler to the hoop. He will often shout "trailer" to alert the player that he is ready for a dump pass backward or a rebound.

Transition: The change from offense to defense, or vice versa. Quickness and alertness here can make a difference.

Trap: Double-teaming a player with the ball, usually in a corner or along the sideline.

Travel: To take two steps without dribbling.

Triple-threat: The balanced offensive or defensive stance from which a player can move in any direction with equal ease.

Turnover: Losing possession to the other team while dribbling or because of a bad pass.

Underneath: The area of the lane underneath or close to the hoop, home to the taller players.

Walking: Taking two steps without a dribble.

Zone: A defense in which each player guards an assigned zone of the court instead of a particular player.

INDEX